The Bible

GOD'S WORD TODAY I

A New Study Guide to the Bible

Emil A. Wcela

The Bible

What It Is and How It Developed

Suggestions for Reflection
by Sr. Jeanne Monahan O.P.

PUEBLO PUBLISHING COMPANY

NEW YORK

Nihil Obstat: *John P. Meier, S.S.D.*
Censor Librorum

Imprimatur: ✠ *James P. Mahoney*
Vicar General,
Archdiocese of New York
August 25, 1975

Design: Frank Kacmarcik, D.F.A.

CONTENTS

PREFACE

Interest in the Scriptures continues to grow. Men and women individually and in groups read, reflect on, discuss, pray from the Bible. I have taught, led, participated in such groups. This participation has convinced me that, despite all the worthwhile material on the Bible already available, there are still gaps to be filled for those people who truly care about the Bible but have had little or no preparation to extract its riches.

Several excellent guides to the Bible exist in the format of booklet series in which each volume provides commentary and explanation on a separate book of the Bible. However, for someone becoming acquainted with the Bible, to work through each book one by one can be a formidable task.

Other books focus on themes and main ideas distilled from the whole Bible. As valuable as such theologies and over-all views are, there is still a need for a familiarity with the *text* of the Bible itself.

In this series, substantial portions of the Scriptures — extensive enough to convey style, language, tone — are the indispensable starting point. Essential background and explanation are provided and the lasting import of the text is suggested. Possibilities for individual or group reflection are offered.

When the reader has completed this series, he will have encountered many themes and main ideas, and this through a selected and guided reading of the text itself. This over-all view can be filled in by further study of the individual books of the Bible.

The general plan emerges from a listing of the titles in this series. It is my strong recommendation that anyone using the series begin with Volume I. If the principles presented there are grasped, the spadework will be done for understanding what follows.

"Indeed, God's word is living and effective, sharper than any two-edged sword. It penetrates and divides soul and spirit, joints and marrow; it judges the reflections and thoughts of the heart" (Hebrews 4:12).

CHAPTER I

THE BIBLE AS THE WORD OF GOD

"In His goodness and wisdom, God chose to reveal Himself
and to make known the hidden purpose of His will (cf. Eph.
1:9) by which through Christ, the Word made flesh, man has
access to the Father in the Holy Spirit and comes to share in
the divine nature (cf. Eph. 2:18; 2 Pet. 1:4). Through this
revelation, therefore, the invisible God (cf. Col. 1:15; 1 Tim.
1:17) out of the abundance of His love speaks to men as
friends (cf. Ex. 33:11; Jn. 15:14-15) and lives among them
(cf. Bar. 3:38), so that He may invite and take them into
fellowship with Himself. This plan of revelation is realized
by deeds and words having an inner unity: the deeds wrought
by God in the history of salvation manifest and confirm the
teaching and realities signified by the words, while the words
proclaim the deeds and clarify the mystery contained in them.
By this revelation then, the deepest truth about God and the
salvation of man is made clear to us in Christ who is the Medi-
ator and at the same time the fullness of all revelation."
Vatican II: Dogmatic Constitution on Divine Revelation, n. 2.

EXPECTATIONS

What do you expect to get when you begin turning the pages
of *Gone With the Wind?*

Are you looking for a glimpse into life in the South during
the Civil War period? Or do you examine the book with the
eyes of an historian, trying to piece together an accurate description of a crucial period in American history?

Is it the characters you are really interested in, Scarlet O'Hara and Rhett Butler and their friends and enemies and the complexity of their lives? Might you possibly be trying to learn something about writing style from the way Margaret Mitchell has put her work together?

Perhaps all you want is some entertainment and relaxation.

Depending on what you expect, reading *Gone With the Wind* will be a joy or a disappointment.

History in the strict sense of the word, it is not. It is a novel built around some historical events. For history of the Civil War, there are writers like Bruce Catton.

Neither is it a sociological study of the South, though it does convey the atmosphere of plantation owners and slaves and carpet-baggers.

Gone With the Wind is the creation of the mind of a talented woman. It is a novel, true in its own way. This way is not the way of history or sociology but an imaginative reconstruction of how a circle of human beings acted in a period of their lives affected by a great historical event, the Civil War.

All that can reasonably be expected of *Gone With the Wind,* or any book or work of art, of indeed any product, is that it live up to the purpose and standard it sets for itself.

WHAT DOES THE BIBLE THINK IT IS DOING

As we approach the Bible, what can we reasonably expect of it? Most of us have formed some ideas of what the Bible is. It's very important to try to find out if what *we think* the Bible is corresponds to what the *Bible thinks* it is.

THE HOLY GOD

The fundamental characteristic of God in the Old Testament is his holiness.

"Holy" has a special meaning. Not something that shines very brightly, or someone who walks around with eyes cast down and hands folded. When applied to God, "Holy" is a statement of what God is like compared to man.

Man dies. God lives forever. Man is hemmed in by his allotted years of life, his special place in time and land, his limited intelligence and physical powers. God is not boxed in. Man has dreams he knows he can never fulfill. God is the perfection of life. Man sins, hurts himself and others by his selfishness and petty self-seeking. God is Good.

For the Scriptures to call God, "Holy", is another way of saying that God is Other. God is different from man and all that man experiences of limitation, frustration, weakness, mortality.

THE PROBLEM WITH BEING HOLY

Precisely this quality of God, that he stands over against the weakness and all-too-obvious humanity of man, causes a problem.

If God is Life and Goodness and Fullness and Happiness, all the things that man yearns for, is God not by this very fact so far out of reach that man can never touch his kind of life?

How can God, Life in its fullness, ever be known by man? Here we use the word, "know," in the biblical sense - not merely a proper cubby-holing of ideas and information but a total relationship between two persons. In this sense, the Bible can speak of a man "knowing" a woman when it refers to sexual relations because this involves a total "knowing," a full relationship of mind and body. How can the lives of God and man come together?

Obviously, God must make some movement, some gesture toward man if man is to cross the great chasm that keeps him from the richness of life he aches for.

THE WORD OF GOD

The Scriptures say over and over again that God gets involved with man through his word. God enters into man's affairs and offers himself and what he is through his word.

But what does "Word" mean? How does the Bible understand this combination of letters? What does reflection on our own experience show us about "word"?

THE WORD AS REVEALING

No man speaks without uncovering his life to those listening to him. Certainly *what* he says will help others know something about his attitudes, his ideas, his values, his sense of humor, etc. If a man says , "I like candied apples," there is some insight into what makes him tick, even on this rather insignificant level. If he says, "I am against all taxes," he gives another clue into the tangle of emotions, beliefs and experiences that make him the individual he is.

But the word does not reveal only through what is said. *How* a man says something also reveals what he is. Certain accents used to be very hard to conceal. Remember the "Brooklyn" accent and the southern drawl? By the way he speaks, a man often conveys what part of the country he comes from. His choice of words, the way he expresses himself, will often communicate a great deal about the extent and type of his education - whether he finished fourth grade or four years of post-graduate study, whether he is accustomed to speaking much or little, how much imagination he has, etc.

These observations on a very basic human experience help us understand what happens in the Scriptures which contain the "word of God."

God's word reveals him. What he says and the way he says it tears away something of the mystery between God and man, puts man in touch with God and God in touch with man.

Recent history has demonstrated all too forcefully that the word has power. Adolf Hitler could spark a whole nation to war by the appeal of his flaming speeches. Then the Age of the Bullhorn came upon us. Picketers, protesters, rally-ers of all shapes, sizes, sexes and schemes expect to stir support by the volume and intensity of their slogans, if not by the worth of their causes.

Politicians work their speeches up to a "Do we want . . .? " so that the audience can be moved to thunder back, "Yes! " or "No! " or whatever the programmed answer is.

God's word, like man's, has power. The force of his personality pushes out into the area of history.

This power in God's word is aimed in a purposeful direction.

God's word creates. Genesis 1 has the story of creation in which a recurrent theme is the power of God's word.

"God said, 'Let there be light,' and there was light . . . God said, 'Let the earth bring forth vegetation' . . . And so it happened . . . God said, 'Let the earth bring forth all kinds of living creatures' . . . And so it happened."

Psalm 33 sings of the power of God's word.
"By the word of the Lord the heavens were made;
by the breath of his mouth all their host."

The reality of God's power in creation is not simply to be marvelled at and then left. Nor does knowing about it provide us with a scientific tidbit to snack on.

Creation is a continuous process in which God not only brings into being a universe which was not previously there, but molds a history, a life story that will ultimately bring man to God.

This final goal of God's creative activity is expressed in the words of St. Paul in the Letter to the Romans (8.19-21). "Indeed, the whole created world eagerly awaits the revelation of the sons of God . . .the world itself will be freed from its slavery to corruption and share in the glorious freedom of the children of God."

This new creation comes about through a history of salvation directed by God's word. Man comes to the Life that is God because God brings him there. The rest of creation is somehow transformed.

The stages in history directed by God's word sometimes seem strange and make sense only when seen in larger perspective. Only with the eyes of faith can one see that any action is really part of God's plan.

About 1250 B. C. the casual onlooker might have seen a caravan of slaves hurrying across the border and away from Egypt and interpreted the sight as just another of the constant breaks that men make toward freedom. The faith of Israel held that it was much more than that.

God had spoken to Moses. "I have witnessed the affliction of my people in Egypt and have heard their cry of complaint against their slave drivers, so I know well what they are suffering. Therefore I have come down to rescue them from the hands of the Egyptians and lead them out of that land into a good and spacious land, a land flowing with milk and honey . . ." (Ex. 3. 7-8).*

History was being made because God was moving it forward by his word. Exactly what God meant to happen through this act of liberation was not yet fully clear. But faith expressed the conviction that God had acted in man's affairs because this was a part of his plan, a plan that would lead ultimately to true freedom, to life with God.

God's word also created a people. The Ten Commandments

* For abbreviations of the Books of the Bible, see pages 60-62.

are called in Hebrew the "Ten Words." These Words make a
unity out of a mixed group of people. They become one because they are to respond to the God who chose them and
acted for them by accepting these words as the direction and
movement of their lives. A "people of the word" comes into
being.

MAN'S RESPONSE

Honest speaking is the beginning of dialogue. God is not some
windy orator who loves empty sound. God speaks in order to
enter into man's life and to make it possible for man to enter
into the divine life.

Two people seated on the 8:15 commuter train, or the flight
to Chicago are two bodies placed next to one another by the
accident of computer seating or available space. While they
remain silent, they are two different worlds, each spinning
in its own orbit, having no influence for good or bad on the
other. But if one of the travellers says, "Good morning. Did
you notice this news in the paper? " something has happened.
The two parties open up to each other, to let their lives be
affected, even on a small scale, by this contact.

We believe that our words can affect others. The teacher who
does not think that his words can create in his students something of his own knowledge, something of the tools with which
he himself has searched for the truth so that they can continue
the search, soon gives up. Or he plods on, but is no longer
teaching.

Parents speak to their children hoping that they will form in
them some of the results of their own experience and values
so that those children will not have to face the crucial decisions
of life empty-handed.

God also speaks to man expecting that his word will take root
in man and affect his life.

7

When God speaks of the meaning of life and its purpose, man's hearing that word involves *faith*. Faith in its most basic sense means the willingness to throw oneself into the interpretation of life that God has spoken because one trusts that God is good, loving, the fullness of life offering himself.

When God speaks of the ways of living out that meaning, what he is expecting as response from his human hearers is *obedience*. This obedience is not fearful cringing before a petty and arbitrary tyrant but the peaceful and free embracing of the way pointed out by a loving God whose interest is the happiness of man.

JESUS AS THE WORD OF GOD

This rich understanding of "word," reflected both in the Old Testament and in human experience, reaches its high point in the New Testament.

The Letter to the Hebrews begins, "In times past, God spoke in fragmentary and varied ways to our fathers through the prophets; in this, the final age, he has spoken to us through his Son . . ."

To say that "God spoke" is to emphasize the personal character of what God is doing.

Something of the character and temperament of a famous artist might be known by looking at his paintings. The skill of a carpenter is demonstrated by what he has built. But this knowledge does not become really personal until one has met the painter or the carpenter and spoken with him.

Man might also know something of God from the works of creation, or from wherever the traces of God are to be found. But God goes far beyong this. He "speaks" to men. Of course, we must avoid a too literal understanding of "speaking" and not imagine it as heavenly sounds thundering over man. "God spoke" means that God has entered and continues to enter into a truly personal relation with men, just as men do when they speak to each other.

This commerce of God with men has been going on for a long time, the author of Hebrews says. In bits and pieces through history, God has been in dialogue with men. But now, God has "spoken" through his Son, which makes our era the definitive period in history in so far as the really crucial issues of existence are concerned. God's speech is no longer partial, a truthful but still wanting expression of himself. His "word," his Son, is a perfect likeness of the Father. The author struggles for ways to express this. He calls the Son, "the reflection of the Father's glory, the exact representation of the Father's being."

The point is that what the Father is, the Son shows, and yet there is a distinction between them.

The Son is the perfect, the exact, the full and complete Word of the Father revealing himself and entering into a relationship with the world of men. If we would see and hear the Father, we look at and listen to his Son.

THE PROLOGUE OF JOHN (JOHN 1. 1-18)

"In the beginning was the Word:
the Word was in God's presence,
and the Word was God."

John's Gospel begins by exclaiming that the Word the Father speaks is also God. "The Word became flesh and made his dwelling among us." The Word became man. God used the most effective way to express himself to men. He "spoke" a "Word" which is the full expression of himself. This "Word" becomes a human being, living with and for men. Jesus is not simply the one who speaks God's word. He is that Word in human form.

The reason for this wonderful manifestation on God's part

is clear. The problem is that 'No one has ever seen God."
No one has ever entered into the kind of relationship with
the Father that is essential for the total and complete fulfillment of man's life.

Therefore, God has stooped into man's history by himself
becoming part of the history. "It is God the only Son,
ever at the Father's side, who has revealed him."

WHERE WE'RE AT

We started with a perhaps impertinent question as to what
the Bible thinks it is. This led us to far-reaching problems
about life. Man can find peace and true joy only when his
life is totally filled. To any one willing to face experience,
it is quite obvious that nothing of what man is and does by
himself can fill his life. So what does satisfy the yearnings
of man must be something "more," something "beyond, "
or in Biblical language, something "holy," something
"other." This is God.

But here frustration begets frustration. A vicious circle
begins its maddening spin. Because the "other" or "holy"
is beyond man's limitations, it can satisfy man. But because
it is "other" or "holy," it is far beyond reach. Man seems
doomed to searching for what he can never have or be.

But the "more" or "other" turns out to be not some im-
personal force, some awesome power, some immense collection of things, but a loving Person who has no wish to
remain aloof or to keep men away from him. The "more"
or "other" which we name God enters into a living, loving
relationship with man. To express the quality of that relationship, the faith of Israel and Christians, using language
which is obviously defective, but all that we have, sings of
God's "speaking" to men.

This speaking of God takes place in the acts of history
which believers interpret as the movement of God revealing

himself and drawing men to himself. Christian faith holds that the high point of this activity of God occurred when his son, his perfect "Word," the fullest expression of all that he is and is doing with men, took human form and lived among men.

The Bible is the story of God's long conversation with men, a conversation which still goes on. It tells of God's efforts to reach out to men and gives the interpretation and meaning of these efforts. It tells of Jesus Christ, God-made-man.

In presenting and interpreting this loving dialogue of God with man, the Bible itself becomes part of that dialogue, an essential part of God speaking to man today, offering himself as the only true satisfaction of human hopes and aspirations.

SUGGESTIONS FOR REFLECTION

1. You have just read a description of God as holy . . . eternal . . . unlimited in intelligence and power . . . the perfection of life . . . all good . . . Other.

To which of these characteristics do you personally relate best?

2. You have also read a description of man as mortal . . . limited to a certain time and space . . . limited in intelligence and physical powers . . . frustrated by unfulfilled dreams . . . capable of sinning and hurting himself and others by selfishness.

Which of these characteristics have you experienced most vividly?

3. Can you recall a time when someone you know revealed himself (his attitudes, ideas, values, humor, etc.) by *what* he said?

4 Recall a time when someone revealed himself (his education, background, nationality, etc.) by *how* he said something.

5. The chapter tells us that words have power. From your experience, describe a time you discovered power in words which you heard or which you spoke yourself.

6. "The reality of God's power in creation is not simply to be marvelled at and then left." Have you ever marvelled at God's power in creation? What caused you to do so? What effect did your "marvelling" have upon you?

7. Describe a time when you realized you had affected someone else's life (a friend, your child, a student, etc.) by your words.

What part did trust and love and faith play in the relationship?

8. Have you ever known a time when a child revealed his parents in some way? When a painting revealed its painter? When a musical composition revealed its composer? Did the revelation occur at once or was it gradual?

9. An ancient Greek philosopher spoke of "the burden of history." The Bible speaks of "the acts of history which believers interpret as the movement of God revealing himself and drawing men to himself."

What basic difference in outlook do you see between the Greek and the biblical vision of history? As you look back on your *life history*, can you think of times God was revealing himself and drawing you to himself? Which viewpoint, the Greek or the biblical, is most often expressed by today's media as they report on world events?

10. It is true that the Bible reveals God, but does it also reveal to us something about people?

11. Describe briefly what you imagine the earth would be like if God had never revealed himself.

12. We understand that God does not speak with a voice or sounds as we do.

Do you find "speaking" a meaningful way of referring to God's self-revelation to us?

CHAPTER II

THE BIBLE AS INSPIRED

"Those divinely revealed realities which are contained and presented in sacred Scripture have been committed to writing under the inspiration of the Holy Spirit. Holy Mother Church, relying on the belief of the apostles, holds that the books of both the Old and New Testament in their entirety, with all their parts, are sacred and canonical because, having been written under the inspiration of the Holy Spirit (cf. Jn. 20:31; 2 Tim. 3:16; 2 Pet. 1:19-21; 3:15-16) they have God as their author and have been handed on as such to the Church herself. In composing the sacred books, God chose men and while employed by Him they made use of their powers and abilities, so that with Him acting in them and through them, they, as true authors, consigned to writing everything and only those things which He wanted."
Vatican II: Dogmatic Constitution on Divine Revelation, n. 11.

"Inspired" as a word serves as a blanket that can cover many situations.

Critics talk about "an inspired painting," "an inspired musical composition," "an inspired book." In the right circles, there might even be conversation about a housewife who turns out "an inspired stew."

The common denominator about all these uses of the word is that there is something special about the product; the painting, the symphony, the book, the stew.

But we have to be more precise than that when we talk

about the Bible as "inspired."

Museums are filled with inspired paintings; libraries, with inspired books; orchestra storerooms, with inspired scores; cookbooks, with inspired recipes.

None of these gets the same kind of reverence, the same kind of attention that the Bible has received through the running centuries.

Evidently, the Bible must be "inspired" in a way which is recognized as different from all other great works of human endeavor.

It will help us to begin with the Bible itself to get this more precise view of the significance of "inspiration."

INSPIRATION IN THE OLD TESTAMENT

There is a Hebrew word, *ruah* (the last "h" is pronounced like the start of gargling) which is translated as "breath" or "wind" or "spirit." That it means all these things is very revealing.

Man's breath cannot be seen. Yet, when no more scientific ways are available to measure whether or not a man is alive, the breath will do. For man not yet advanced enough to know about brain waves and other signals that go by the designation of "vital signs," the life is somehow in the breath. Where there is breath, there is life. Where there is no breath, there is no life. It is as simple as that.

The wind is another mysterious force. In the land which is the home of the Bible, it can come bringing scorching heat that parches and cracks the fields from which the farmer is trying to coax some food. The unbearably warm puffs drive man and beast up to quick temper and down to listless labor.

Or the wind arrives pregnant with the rain that cools the

baked land, turns brown furrows to waving green and assures food for the year.

Both "breath" and "wind" have this in common. They are unseen forces on which life depends. If one cannot picture "breath" or "wind," he can imagine the living man who breathes and rustling acres of grain that the rain wind has mysteriously brought alive.

So the *ruah,* the breath, the wind, is also the "spirit," an intangible life-force that is obvious mostly in the difference in man or nature when the spirit is present and when it is absent.

THE SPIRIT OF GOD

This idea of "spirit" fits God. The way it is applied to other things suggests that the "spirit of God" is the "life-force," for want of a better term, of God himself. The spirit of God should be most evident in what it does.

What does this spirit of God, this life-force, do?

First, let us turn to the Old Testament.

In the story of Moses, just as the Israelites draw near to the Promised Land, Moses is told by God to climb a mountain and look across the Jordan River to the land that his people will soon enter. Moses himself will die before he can lead the people in.

Moses reasons things out with God, treating him as though he may not have thought through what is happening. "May the Lord, the God of the spirits of all mankind, set over the community a man who shall act as their leader in all things, to guide them in all their actions; that the Lord's community may not be like sheep without a shepherd."

God's answer? "Take Joshua, son of Nun, a man of spirit

and lay your hand upon him. Have him stand in the presence of the priest Eleazar and of the whole community, and commission him before their eyes. Invest him with some of your own dignity, that the whole Israelite community may obey him" (Num 27. 16-17, 18-20).

Here, spirit is a power that comes from God and qualifies man for the leadership of God's people.

The stories of the "judges" tell of the Israelites as independent tribes, more or less loosely tied together by a shared faith in Yahweh as their God. There is no standing army to protect them, no central government to solve their problems. The problems they do have, as related in the Book of Judges, consist of raids from neighboring tribes who attack their settlements and carry off their flocks, their crops, their women and children.

In just such a situation, "the Israelites cried out to the Lord (and) he raised up for them a savior, Othniel . . . who rescued them. The spirit of the Lord came upon him . . . When he went out to war, the Lord delivered Cushan-rishathaim, king of Aram, into his power . . . The land was then at rest for forty years . . ." (Jgs 3.7-11).

Never mind for the time being whether the idea of God making men warriors is very attractive. That is a problem for some later reflection. Right now our concern is with the fact that it is the spirit of God which makes this man into a powerful fighter and leader to deliver his people from oppression.

In the second half of the eighth century B.C., the prophet Isaiah described a king in terms that are full of hope for an ideal future.

"The spirit of the Lord shall rest upon him:
a spirit of wisdom and of understanding,
A spirit of counsel and of strength,

a spirit of knowledge and of fear of the Lord . . .
He shall judge the poor with justice,
and decide aright for the land's afflicted . . ."

This is followed by a beautiful description of universal harmony and peace (Is 11.1-9).

Here then is something else the spirit of God does. It fits a man to rule his people with integrity and justice, to bring peace.

Sometime before the destruction of Jerusalem by a Babylonian army in 587 B. C., the prophet Ezekiel is made to see all the evil in the city which is the cause of the inevitable disaster hanging over it. God tells him ". . . Prophesy against them, son of man, prophesy! Then the spirit of the Lord fell upon me, and he told me to say: Thus says the Lord: This is the way you talk, house of Israel, and what you are plotting I well know. You have slain many in this city and have filled the streets with your slain . . . I will bring you out of the city, and hand you over to foreigners, and inflict punishments upon you" (Ez. 11.4-6, 9).

Here, the spirit of God fits Ezekiel to face God's people with their sins and the consequences they can expect from them.

In the Old Testament, what is there in common among leadership, the ability to assemble a make-shift army and guide it to victory, the wise rule of a king, the challenging words of a critic of his society?

All are the result of God's intervention. And in each case, God gets involved to help his people; to give them necessary guidance, to free them from oppression, to provide them with a reign of peace and justice, to make them see how they have turned away from him.

In other words, the Old Testament considers the spirit of

God to be the power, the life-force, the vitality, of God which he somehow pours into men to accomplish his good purposes among them.

All of this helps to fill out what "inspiration" means when applied to the production of the Bible.

To be inspired means to be moved by the living, loving power of God to bring about his aims in the world.

Note how in the examples used there was no mention yet of the spirit of God as an impulse to men to write; only to act, to lead, to rule, to speak. It is within this broad range of divinely directed activity that the stages in the writing of the Old Testament belong.

INSPIRATION IN THE NEW TESTAMENT

INSPIRATION TO SPEAK

The writings of the New Testament continue in the traditional meaning of "inspired."

Mark 12.35-37 relates how while Jesus was teaching in the Temple, he said, "David himself, inspired by the Holy Spirit, said: 'The Lord said to my Lord: Sit at my right hand until I make your enemies your footstool.' "

In a sermon attributed to Paul in the Acts of the Apostles, Paul added one final word: 'The Holy Spirit stated it well when he said to your fathers through the Prophet Isaiah:
"Go to this people and say:
You may listen carefully yet you will never understand" (Acts 28. 25, 26).

David and Isaiah are both characterized as inspired because moved by the spirit of God, but the action to which they are moved is speaking.

Summing up this point of view is the Second Letter of Peter, 1.21, " . . .men impelled by the Holy Spirit have spoken under God's influence,"

INSPIRATION TO WRITE

In a warning against false teachers and doctrines (2 Tim 3. 10-17) Timothy, the young leader of a Christian community is told to rely on the Scriptures (the Old Testament) and the traditional teaching of the apostles for the truth. The passage ends, "All scripture is inspired of God and is useful for teaching — for reproof, correction and training in holiness."

The author here speaks of the Scriptures as "inspired," recognizing that God's life-giving spirit expresses itself in order to accomplish God's saving purposes, through the writing of the Bible.

WHAT INSPIRATION MEANS

What makes the Bible different?   The fact that a God who enters into a loving relationship with men moves men by his power to live, to do, to speak in ways that reveal him.

God Saves. He frees. He rules. He guides. He speaks. And he does this through men whom he fills in a mysterious way with his own power.

This process of being filled or moved with the life or spirit of God can be called inspiration, being "Breathed-into" since this is the literal meaning of the word. One special way in which God has moved men to his work of self-revelation and salvation is the writing of the Bible.

The Bible is different not because of its pious thoughts, or deep theology, or profound insights. These it has, but it is different because in a a way that can be attributed to no other book or work of man, the very life-power of God has been behind its composition.

GOD'S WORK BUT THROUGH MEN

Time now for a word of caution and explanation.

That God is responsible for the Bible, that he is the impulse behind its formation, does not imply magic. Visibly and measurably, the process of creating the Bible is no different from the usual labor that goes into the composition of a work of literature.

It took well over 1300 years for the Bible to get put between its present covers. The people who produced it differed in their backgrounds, in their education, in the depth of their religious insight, in what they were trying to communicate, in their own personal religious experience.

The Bible includes a staggering variety of material, from hymns to love songs; from chronicles of the reign of a king to shouts of victory after a battle; from laws to legends about folk heroes; from letters to angry sermons to a sinful people.

Not to recognize this great variety is to oversimplify and so to misunderstand God's ways of working among men. To be avoided is the lurking suspicion that there is a kind of God language in the Bible; that God, in the making of the Bible, had men speak and think and write in some other way than normal. A few examples might help.

HOSEA

Hosea lived during the middle of the eighth century before Christ. Two vivid experiences marked his life.

One could hardly have been more personal and intimate. He was married to a prostitute. This woman, Gomer, eventually left Hosea. Despite the humiliation and pain she caused him, Hosea found that he could not deny the love that throbbed in him.

The other experience, also personal but involving many more

people, was the general corruption and decay of religious life and social justice among his fellow countrymen. They abandoned the worship of Yahweh, the God of Israel, to take after false gods. They embraced the orgiastic forms of worship that suited these gods.

Further, as always happens when men tangle their relationship with God, they perverted their responsibilities and respect for one another. The rich got richer by bribing corrupt judges to decide cases in their behalf. The religious and political leaders offered no challenge to the corruption around them but were carried along with it, being only too willing to pander to the wealthy and powerful. Money, power, pleasure, became the only incentives for living, no matter who got crushed in the scramble.

Many men and women have had the experience of an unfaithful spouse. Many men and women have lived in degenerate and festering societies. Hosea was moved by God to put these two experiences together for a totally unexpected glimpse of God.

Just as Hosea could not stop loving his wife despite her infidelity, God cannot stop loving his people despite their infidelity. In each case, some kind of correction and testing of the unfaithful partner is called for but what moves all along is the overwhelming love that Hosea has for his wife and Yahweh for his people.

When Hosea spoke about God's relationship to his people, he expressed himself in language that flowed from his own hurt. God's people is a "harlot," as is Hosea's wife. Both are chasing after "lovers," from whom they expect good things. When the people finally turn back to God, they will again call him, "my husband," as Gomer will say of Hosea the day she returns.

To put it briefly, Hosea speaks about God in language that reflects his own time, his own deeply personal marital ex-

perience, his religious experience. His language, his insight,
his message, his plea, are all conditioned by these. Yet
God is behind it all.

WISDOM

About 650 years after Hosea's time — the date would be about
100 B.C. — the scene is no longer the kingdom of Israel, but
Egypt. The city of Alexandria is a brilliant center of culture.
All the beautiful people come here to hear the latest in fads
and fashions, to pursue serious studies, to be exposed to
advanced ideas.

In the city there is a Jewish colony, much troubled by the
flashiness around it. There is so much that looks attractive
in the new. The old faith of Israel in its God is surely out
of date. Now is the time to give all that up, to accept the
brave new world being fashioned by the philosophers and
wise men.

But a voice is raised, the voice of an educated Jewish believer.
He reminds his people that the answers to life, its problems,
its hopes, are brought no nearer by the philosophical specu-
lations, no matter how profound. All still hangs together in
God.

The author hides his own name and identity by putting his
work forward as the words of the glorious king, Solomon —
a common enough writing device in those days.

The book is framed in the language and style of the Greek
speakers of Alexandria, reflects the ideas of the time, faces a
critical situation of the time.

But the faith in God and the answers to man's quest about
life remain a permanent challenge to men of all times.

PAUL

Paul's letters are about 150 years later than the Book of Wisdom, about 800 years later than the words of Hosea. Born a Jew, he studied under a famous rabbi in Jerusalem and lived out exemplary Judaism. But he also spent much of his life in the wider world colored by the cultures of Greece, Rome and Asia Minor.

Most important of all, although early a persecutor of the Christians, he experienced the Risen Christ in a way that changed his whole life and turned him into a dedicated and burning missionary for the Lord.

His letters were written to the young Christian communities, mostly in Greece and Asia Minor. They dealt with theological questions and practical problems peculiar to the times and circumstances. Should women wear head coverings in church? Is there too much disorder in a free-wheeling liturgy where people stand and sit and sing and talk as the spirit moves them? Should a Christian who has a grievance against another Christian take him to court when one considers that these courts are presided over by non-Christians?

From these specific problems, Paul moves to the deep and enduring principles that are to be the constant guide for Christian life. In expressing these principles, Paul used the language of a Jewish rabbi, of a Greek philosopher, of a Christian teacher.

GOD THROUGH HOSEA, WISDOM, PAUL

These are only three examples from the Bible, yet they surely make the point. Inspiration, being moved by God, does not mean that a person loses his individuality. Being inspired by no means reduces Hosea, the author of Wisdom, or Paul, to a kind of uniform "Inspired Author," each expressing exactly the same ideas in exactly the same way. Inspiration does not mean that a man speaking in the year 750 B. C. will use the same language as a man 650 years later, any more than Shakespeare used modern English.

Inspiration does not mean that the personal religious experiences of an individual lose their meaning and the individual becomes a lifeless typewriter or fountain pen in God's hand. Rather through personal experiences and reflection on them guided by the Holy Spirit, the individual comes to his particular vision of God.

Inspiration does not keep an author from being a bad speller, or a poor speaker, or an inaccurate historian. Inspiration does not give an author a scientific knowledge beyond his time, or polish his literary style when he has had no education.

Inspiration is God working with and through all kinds of men to communicate what he wanted communicated.

ONE AUTHOR TO A BOOK?

Even saying this much still does not exhaust the complexity of the inspiration of the Bible.

This complexity remains to be faced in the fact that for many of the books of the Bible, there is not just one author. The creation of a book of the Bible was most often not due simply to the effort of one man determined to write about God's moves in history.

Take, for example the well-known stories of Samson, including the notorious episode with Delilah (Jgs 13-16).

Samson belongs in the period between 1200 and 1050 B. C. Some Israelites had pushed into the Promised Land to be joined by local inhabitants who were willing to accept their God, Yahweh. However, there was still no central government, no uniform body of law, no stable defensive system for the tribes that made up Israel. Each lived in its own area, tried to make its settlement permanent, did its best to ward off the attacks of outsiders, moved to take pockets of non-Israelites living in its territory.

One such tribe was Dan. The greatest threat to this tribe was the people called the Philistines who had a firm foothold and comparatively strong organization along the Mediterranean coast of Palestine. The people of Dan found themselves under constant pressure from the Philistines. There was almost continuous battle, at least by way of skirmishes between small bands of rough and ready fighters.

By whacking the Philistines a few times, a man of Dan, Samson, acquired a reputation and the status of hero. The stories of his exploits were repeated in the camps and settlements of the Danites. They cheered their hero as they related how he made life miserable for the common enemy. In the telling, the stories grew more impressive, more and more entertaining, as hero stories will. Samson killed 1000 men with the jawbone of an ass. He caught 300 foxes, set lighted torches to their tails and sent them running through the wheat fields of the Philistines, thus cleverly destroying their crops.

At his wedding feast, after marriage to a Philistine woman, he made a bet of thirty fine suits of clothes. The wager was that the young Philistine men with him at the feast could not answer within seven days a riddle he posed. They accepted the bet and, failing to solve the riddle, they prevailed upon his wife to use her charms and persistence to wheedle the answer from Samson. On the seventh day, they smugly tossed at Samson the solution gotten through treachery.

Was our hero beaten? By no means!

He went to another Philistine town, killed thirty men and despoiled them of their clothes to pay the bet.

A grisly turn certainly! But this is the stuff that stories of folk heroes are made of. One can almost imagine the harried Danites smiling and applauding as the local storyteller emphatically related how crafty Samson got the better of their mortal enemies once again.

This story, part of the heritage of one tribe of Israel, was passed on from one generation to another. But then Israel changed. No longer independent tribes loosely held together by a common faith in Yahweh, it became a nation. Many decades later, as the people of the nation looked back on these stories of Samson, they understood them as part of their common history, as part of a campaign that went on in many places over many years through which the Israelites finally won possession of the Promised Land.

Samson was understood better as one of those used by God to give the Land to his people.

In time, this story of Samson was strung together with other stories of local heroes from other tribes to reconstruct a history of the whole people, which the faith of Israel believed was guided by God.

Something similar happens in American history when the history of one state, Massachusetts for example, an independent colony at first, has to be recognized as also playing an integral part in the history of the country that would eventually come into being, the United States.

The Samson and other hero stories were finally included in a full-scale history of Israel made up of the Books of Joshua, Judges, 1-2 Samuel, 1-2 Kings. For this final step, the story was once again adapted, rearranged, given new theological interpretations to fit into its new setting.

This process, from the actual events of the life of Samson, whatever they might have been, to the final appearance of the stories in the Book of Judges as it is today, took something like 600 years.

If we think of the biblical books as having an author, who was the author of the Samson stories?

Was it the minstrel who sang about Samson around tribal campfires? The unknown persons who first wrote them down? The compilers who first included them with other hero stories? The theologians who first gave them a theological meaning in the comprehensive plan of God for Israel? The editor who gave them the final form we have now?

The reality of inspiration would be impoverished if we tried to look for one person and say that he and he alone was inspired. All the people mentioned played some part in the fact that the Bible contains the stories of Samson.

THE GOSPELS

The Gospels reflect the same complex procedure. Jesus wrote nothing. There is no indication that Jesus material was being written during his life time. Even after his death, his message and teaching were preserved and presented not through written gospels but through the living memory of Jesus being preached by his followers.

Beginning some thirty years after the death of Jesus, the gospel writers gathered traditions about Jesus, some oral, some now written, which were the faith heritage of the communities they belonged to. They selected and arranged from this material, aiming to present Jesus and his message from their particular point of view.

Who was inspired in this process? Only the gospel writers? But what about the earliest apostles and preachers who first carried the message of Jesus to the world? What about the little pockets of Christians who preserved this preaching? What about those who started to put some of this preaching and teaching into written form even before the gospels were written? Some of this material was used by the Evangelists. Would it not be too narrow to consider only the gospel writers as inspired and to leave outside the movement of God's Spirit all the others who were in some way responsible for what the gospels eventually contained?

28

UNDERSTANDING INSPIRATION

It should be clear by now that inspiration is a very complex phenomenon. We would be fooling ourselves and short-changing the mystery of inspiration if we ever thought we had gotten to the stage of saying, "So that's what inspiration is! "

However, if complete understanding is not possible, some comprehension is.

1. Inspiration works primarily in and through the community of those who believe. The process of understanding God more deeply through his actions in history for and through men and of communicating this understanding takes place especially in the life of a people called by God. In their experience, in their reflection on that experience, in their awareness of their traditions, the community, guided by the Spirit, deepens its relationship with its God.

But within that community are certain individuals who by what they say, or what they do, or what they write, reflect and focus what the community believes. These individuals would make no sense outside the community.

Sometimes they express what the community believes, and in what they say or do or write, the community recognizes that this is a true reflection of its belief.

We might take an example from our own history. The Declaration of Independence represents the touch of Thomas Jefferson. But in it, he was expressing, in his own words and his own style, the feelings of many of the American colonists. They accepted his written formulation as the expression of the basic beliefs that united them.

So, the Gospel of Matthew is the expression of the faith of an early Christian community about the meaning of Jesus and his work. The Gospel came from believers of

Jewish background. The author did not create his Gospel from nothing but from the faith and the way of expressing it that he was familiar with. And then, the believing community recognized his expression and arrangement of its beliefs as an authentic one.

A biblical author can be related to his community in another way. He may stand against it and challenge its life as a perversion of the true faith.

The prophets were just such men. Most often, their message was a fearsome criticism of the shabby state of the faith of the community. They saw the life of the community as weak, self-seeking, hypocritical.

But even here, their criticism did not come out of simply personal attitudes or convictions. It was based on the prophet's understanding of the authentic traditions of the community. In other words, the prophet, guided by the Spirit and led to new insights spoke out of his sense of what the real life of the community ought to be. But he would have had no sense of that authentic faith were there not an ongoing awareness of God's relationship to men that the prophet himself had experienced in the life of the community, or at least in some segment of it. And he would not have spoken were it not for the community which he saw veering from the true ways of God with man.

2. Does the author of a biblical work know that he is inspired?

If this means, "Does he have some mystical experience? Are his days filled with visions and divine words echoing thunderously around him? " the answer would have to be, "In almost all cases, No! "

There is no indication that the men of the Bible spoke or wrote in ways which were different from the ways men ordinarily speak or write.

30

However, it can legitimately be presumed that the authors of the Bible were aware that what they were saying or writing did indeed reflect the belief of a community. They understood themselves as expressing the true faith of the believing community.

3. If the process of the formation of the Bible was as complicated as has been suggested, then the gift or charism of inspiration is indeed many-faceted. The Spirit, through this gift, guided the speaking and writing of poetry, history, proverbs, love songs. He was behind a process of gathering, editing, remembering, material both written and spoken. He moved men to select material out of much that must have been available, to arrange it, to adapt it.

4. This might seem to make the power of the Spirit so diverse that it becomes nothing, like water spilling out of a rusty pail through a hundred holes. Not so! The point is that the production of the Scriptures was such a varied process that any attempt to understand inspiration as only one impulse, one movement, one activity, is such an oversimplification as to be of no help at all.

It would be like defining publishing a newspaper as "The local newspaper is published when the newsboy drops it at my door." Such a description leaves out the process of newsgathering by reporters and news agencies, the editing of such reports, the storing of information for later use, the formation and carrying out of an editorial policy, etc.

At the same time, the inspiration of the actual scriptural writer is not reduced to nothing. He is the object of a special movement, a special grace from God, whether or not he is aware of this impulse and the special role that he is playing in God's plan.

CONCLUSIONS

Biblical inspiration refers to the whole process, as complex as life itself, by which the Spirit-guided communities of Israel and early Christianity reflected on their histories, saw in these histories the self-revelation of God; preserved, selected, adapted, arranged and finally put in written form, through privileged members of the community, their understanding of this self-revelation.

The purpose of the final product of this process, the Bible, is the understanding of God and of man in relation to God that comes from contemplating the special moments in God's commerce with man. This is especially true of the New Testament which is the record of the high point of God's loving entrance into the affairs of men.

However, the Bible is not the plaything of antiquarians and historians. It is still the living word of God to all men at all times. It speaks to men today. It speaks in the same way that it was formed, in and through the community and guided by the Holy Spirit. It can be heard in its fullness only in and through the community and under the guidance of the Spirit.

"Sacred tradition and sacred Scripture form one sacred deposit of the word of God, which is committed to the Church. Holding fast to this deposit, the entire holy people united with their shepherds remain always steadfast in the teaching of the apostles, in the common life, in the breaking of the bread, and in prayers (cf. Acts 2, 42, Greek text), so that in holding to, practicing, and professing the heritage of the faith, there results on the part of the bishops and faithful a remarkable common effort.

"The task of authentically interpreting the word of God, whether written or handed on, has been entrusted exclusively to the living teaching office of the Church, whose authority is exercised in the name of Jesus Christ. This teaching office is not above the word of God, but serves it, teaching only what has been handed on, listening to it devoutly, guarding it scrupulously, and explaining it faithfully by divine commission and with the help of the Holy Spirit; it draws from this one deposit of faith everything which it presents for belief as divinely revealed.

"It is clear, therefore, that sacred tradition, sacred Scripture, and the teaching authority of the Church, in accord with God's most wise design, are so linked and joined together that one cannot stand without the others, and that all together and each in its own way under the action of the one Holy Spirit contribute effectively to the salvation of souls."
Vatican II: Dogmatic Constitution on Divine Revelation, n. 10.

SUGGESTIONS FOR REFLECTION

1. Have you ever seen a painting, or sculpture, or piece of architecture, or heard music, or read a book, that was so special that you thought of it as "inspired"?

2. Describe an experience you have had in which the spirit ("breath" or "wind") was absent in man or nature (a flower, animal, garden, etc.)

3. Describe an experience you have had in which you definitely knew the spirit ("breath" or "wind") was present in man or nature.

4. In the Bible we see God's life-giving spirit expressing itself in leadership, wise ruling, speaking in prophecy to criticize wrongs, and in writing.

Can you mention other ways the life-giving force or spirit expresses itself today to accomplish God's saving purpose? Are these expressions of spirit considered inspired in the same way as the Bible?

5. How can each of us, despite differences in language, background, nationality, age, sex, reveal God today to others?

6. Hosea and Paul each came to his own particular vision of God through reflection on his own personal experiences in the light of his religious traditions and guided by the Holy Spirit.

What is this telling you about how to find your own vision of God and meaning of life? What would it require of you from day to day?

7. In 1 Cor 12.7, we are told, "To each person the manifestation of the Spirit is given for *the common good.*"

What relationship does this have to our previously stressed emphasis on the good of our own soul, and personal sanctification as the goal of life? Can the two ideas be reconciled?

8. The story of Samson seems to have had many authors in its development. Can you recall any stories or songs or legends in history that might have developed in a similar way?

9. Read the story of Samson in the Bible (Jgs 13-16). Try to locate which aspects belong to legend, which might have been added by theologians.

10. When we read the Bible, why is it important that we become familiar with the interpretations given by the Church to the inspired readings?

CHAPTER III

THE BIBLE AS TRUE

"Therefore, since everything asserted by the inspired authors or sacred writers must be held to be asserted by the Holy Spirit, it follows that the books of Scripture must be acknowledged as teaching firmly, faithfully, and without error that truth which God wanted put into the sacred writing for the sake of our salvation.

"However, since God speaks in sacred Scripture through men in human fashion, the interpreter of sacred Scripture, in order to see clearly what God wanted to communicate to us, should carefully investigate what meaning the sacred writers really intended, and what God wanted to manifest by means of their words.

"In sacred Scripture, therefore, while the truth and holiness of God always remains intact, the marvelous 'condescension of eternal wisdom is clearly shown, that we may learn the gentle kindness of God, which words cannot express, and how far He has gone in adapting His language with thoughtful concern for our weak human nature.' For the words of God, expressed in human language, have been made like human discourse, just as of old the Word of the eternal Father, when he took to Himself the weak flesh of humanity, became like other men." *Vatican II: Dogmatic Constitution on Divine Revelation.* Excerpts from nn. 11, 12 and 13.

The Bible receives more and more emphasis as a source of instruction both in and outside the liturgy, as one of the ways in which God speaks to the world, as the starting point

35

for prayer for both individuals and groups. At just about the same pace, it becomes a more and more perplexing document for those who would like to read and learn from it and nourish their life of faith.

Parents with children in Catholic schools or religious instruction classes have been shaken by the often over-simplified and misunderstood statements their offspring bring home.

"In religion class, Mrs. Jones said that there were no Adam and Eve."

"Sister said that the Epiphany Wise Men may just be a story."

The more sophisticated may have stopped conversations with questions about the virginity of Mary or the physical resurrection of Jesus.

Unfortunately, sometimes statements and questions like these are put forth by teachers who understand them poorly. Sometimes they represent a distortion where the shock effect gets in the way of the central message of faith. And sometimes they have just gotten terribly mangled in passing from teacher's mind, through his mouth, into Junior's ear, through his brain, out of his mouth, into Dad's or Mother's ear.

There are many legitimate questions that have to be raised. The creation story, the rich teaching of the Adam and Eve account are not easy to understand. The story of Jonah is generally accepted by scholars as a parable with a message none the less profound for not being literal history. The debate over the possibility of knowing *exactly* what Jesus said and did, using the Gospels as sources, continues.

Such discussion, freely publicized in the popular press and in lectures meant for general consumption, leaves even the best-intentioned people bewildered and in despair about how much stock they should put in the Bible.

It is essential, therefore, that we consider very carefully
what has been a fundamental belief of the Christian community, that the Bible is true. From formulating its belief
that the Bible is true, the Church, in dialogue with God and
human history, has grown to a deeper understanding of
how the Bible is true.

THE HISTORY OF THE DISCUSSION

The meaning of the basic belief that the Scriptures share in
the truth of God himself has had to be spelled out in the
context of controversy. Attacks on the truth of the Bible
have come fast and furious from the very beginning. The
attacks and questions have been directed at those areas that
the spirit, the state of development, and the main pre-occu-
pations of each age have seen as especially weak and ques-
tionable.

THE BIBLE AGAINST ITSELF

The earliest discussion took place with critics who probed
at what they considered the contradictions and inconsistencies within the Scriptures. Thus, in the third century, a
critic of Christianity named Porphyry emphasized the lack
of agreement he discerned between Matthew's Gospel, in
which it seems that the Holy Family left for Egypt the same
night that Jesus was born, and Luke's, which has the family
still in Jerusalem forty days later for the presentation in the
Temple. He finds an incoherent and contradictory account
of the passion in the Gospels because according to Matthew,
Jesus cries out on the cross, "My God, my God, why have
you forsaken me? " According to Luke, "Father, into your
hands I commend my spirit." According to John, "Now it
is finished."

We might add still other examples of places where the Bible
seems to disagree with itself. In the Noah story, Genesis
7.17 says, "The flood continued upon the earth for forty
days," but in 7.24, "The waters maintained their crest over

the earth for one hundred and fifty days."

The Books of Joshua and Judges both tell of the conquest of the Holy Land by the Israelites. But some of the areas that Joshua affirms were conquered, Judges admits remained outside the control of the Israelites.

This list might go on and on.

In this type of discussion, the early Christian teachers and leaders affirmed the truth of the Scriptures through thick and thin. In 405, in a letter to St. Jerome, St. Augustine stated his principle for dealing with difficult cases.

"Not one of their (the canonical books of Scripture) authors has erred in writing anything at all. If I do find anything in those books which seems contrary to the truth, I decide that either the text is corrupt, or the translator did not follow what was really said, or that I failed to understand it."

This is the solid tradition of the first centuries of the Church. The possibility of error of any kind in the Bible was ruled out.

THE BIBLE IN A SCIENTIFIC AGE

In the 17th century, the battleground shifted. No longer was the trustworthiness of the Bible questioned only in terms of its own internal inconsistencies. Now the blossoming scientific spirit began to find areas of conflict with the word of God.

The Galileo affair (1616) was partially a question of the truth of the Bible. The judges of the Inquistion found Galileo's ideas about the earth revolving around the sun at fault because, they claimed, the Scriptures teach that the earth is the center of the universe.

Ecclesiastes 1.4 maintains, "One generation passes and other comes, but the world forever stays." This "staying" involves not only time but place. How then can the world revolve around the sun?

The development of modern historical writing in the 19th century compounded the problems for the truth of the Bible. If history is conceived as the accurate and precise account of events as they happened, in so far as this can be established from trustworthy records, official documents, etc., how could the Gospels, for example, be accepted as serious history?

Matthew's Sermon on the Mount, three chapters long, seems to be Luke's sermon "at a level stretch," less than one chapter long.

Matthew lists eight beatitudes while Luke lists four beatitudes and four "woes." Luke's version of the Lord's Prayer is shorter than Matthew's by two petitions, leaving out "your will be done on earth as it is in heaven," and "deliver us from the evil one."

Mark speaks of the cure of *one* blind man while Jesus was *leaving* Jericho. Matthew indicates that it was *two* blind men who were cured when Jesus had *left* Jericho. Luke refers to *one* blind man, cured while Jesus *came to* Jericho.

Surely the scientific historian trying to paint an accurate and precise picture will give up in impatience.

ATTEMPTS TO RECONCILE THE TRUTH OF THE BIBLE WITH THE FINDINGS OF THE SCIENTIFIC AGE

During the 19th century, defenders of the Bible tried to speak to the objections being raised.

An approach that came to be known as "concordism" recognized the truth being discovered in the amazing advances of science but at the same time insisted that the Bible was also presenting the truth, even in scientific matters. It was all a matter of understanding the scientific teaching of the Bible properly.

So, the Bible speaks of creation in seven days. Science indicates that the formation of the universe happened over millions of years. Since both are true, the Bible must be referring not to seven days of twenty-four hours each but to seven periods of time of indefinite length, seven eons, which could include the millions of years the scientists insisted were necessary for the universe to come into being.

This approach collapses in the face of the almost incredible advances in scientific information with which the Bible's views could in no way be reconciled.

There can be no denying that the Old Testament shares the views of the cosmos that were accepted in its own time. The earth, flat, pancake-like, floats on water. This earth is covered over by a kind of upside-down bowl which touches the horizon all around. Sun, moon, stars, hang from this bowl. Water flows over the bowl on the outside. Rain is some of this water let in through openings in the otherwise solid dome. Rivers and streams are water from under the earth breaking through in fixed places.

As far as the seven days of creation being seven vague and long periods of time, this well-intentioned explanation does not survive even the test of a careful reading of the text of Genesis. On each day of creation, Genesis says, "Evening came and morning followed." The author was certainly thinking of days of twenty-four hours just like the ones he knew, divided into day and night.

Faced with these developments, from about 1850 on, some Catholic writers in England, France and Germany were willing, for the first time, to allow that there were errors which were believed and affirmed by the writers of the Scriptures.

40

Although their presentations took a wide variety of forms, these Catholics, among them Cardinal Newman, claimed that secular science and even history were not the main concern of the inspired authors. Matters that have to do with faith and morals are true. Those that are not of faith and morals are not inspired, or if inspired, are not guaranteed as true.

Most of this kind of explanation which tried to come to terms with problems revolving around the truth of the Bible by placing some kind of limit on its extension ground to a halt when condemned in 1907 in the course of the movement and controversy in the Church known as "Modernism."

However, it would be wrong to imagine that only our enlightened times recognize the problems involved in taking the Bible absolutely literally in all areas, especially in matters of science. Over 1500 years ago, St. Augustine had stated, to those who wished to find in the Scriptures divine teaching on the make-up of the world, that the Holy Spirit had no intention of teaching about things which do not serve the salvation of men. The same Augustine also wrote that the Lord never said he was sending the Paraclete to teach men about the movements of the sun and moon. "He (the Lord) wished to make Christians, not mathematicians," says Augustine.

This insight into the relation between the Bible and the physical sciences received official recognition in the 1893 encyclical of Pope Leo XIII, *Providentissimus Deus.*

Augustine's principle is cited and accepted. The Scriptures do not intend to teach those things which are of no value to our salvation. Further, what is said about "science" is based on the observations of the men of the time when the Bible was being formed. This is known as "science according to appearances."

The sky is described as an upside-down bowl, solid, because to a man gazing at the wonders of the world without modern scientific instruments and background, the sky does look like a bowl resting on the horizon all round.

Some biblical commentators tried to use the same general principles to solve the historical discrepancies in the Bible. The Book of Daniel, for instance, has the famous story of the handwriting on the wall. During a banquet given by "King Belshazzar," a mysterious hand appears and writes three words on the wall. Only Daniel can interpret them as foretelling the impending destruction of the kingdom of King Belshazzar.

The historical problem consists in the fact that the Book of Daniel puts this man, Belshazzar, on the stage about forty years before he actually made his appearance. Further, he was never really a king.

For this type of situation, interpreters spoke of "history according to appearances" to parallel "science according to appearances." By this they meant that the authors of the Bible could go along with the unsophisticated and un-critical opinions current among the ordinary people of their time without passing judgment on the objective his-torical truth that might or might not be behind these opinions.

This explanation ran into difficulties that required its refining and elaboration, because the objections were well-taken. Science may not be essential for the faith of Christians, but history is. Judaism and Christianity are based on certain historical events; the Exodus from Egypt, the life, death and resurrection of Jesus. If these central events never took place, there would be lacking a basis on which to demand faith in the liberating and loving God. More on this later.

DIRECTIONS IN RECENT EXPLANATIONS OF THE TRUTH OF THE BIBLE

Recent Catholic thinkers who have wrestled with the issue of the truth of the Bible present a number of principles that bring us a long way in understanding what we mean when we say that "The Bible is true."

1. The formal object of the Bible is to reveal the saving activity of God, especially as it reaches its high point in Jesus Christ.

The truth of any communication — writing, speech, sign — depends on what the communicator wants to get across. The goal, the purpose, that the speaker has in mind is his *formal object*. Simply put, the formal object is what the author *means* to say by what he says.

A scientist, just returned home from the laboratory where he has been studying moon rocks, tells his three-year old son a bedtime story which includes "and the cow jumped over the moon." This is not the kind of information he would include in his report for NASA. His purpose in the laboratory is to assemble scientific data, as objective and as carefully measured as possible. In his son's bedroom, he has another goal altogether, to entertain his delighted son with stories of a never-never land. In each case, his formal object is different. He means to accomplish different purposes.

To write in his scientific report that the cow jumped over the moon would make him a poor scientist, or indeed a liar, if there is no data for cows jumping over the moon, and if the indications are that this is impossible. To tell his son that the cow jumped over the moon by way of imaginative entertainment does not open the scientist to charges of incompetence or lying.

Applying this to the Bible and following the lead given in the statements of St. Augustine already seen, the aim of the Bible is primarily to reveal the saving work of God, especially as this is manifested in Jesus Christ. Scientific statements, assertions about culture, history, etc., are to be scrutinized from this point of view. The ultimate question to be asked of any part of the Bible is, "What does this teach about God and his loving, saving relationship to man? "

This does not imply that the Bible can be broken into segments, some of which have to do with God's saving activity and so are true, and some of which do not and so need not be true. All the Bible is true, but it is true from one particular direction, i. e., for communicating to man the loving and saving God, his activity for man, his revelation of the meaning of man's life.

2. In the Bible, "truth" has a special meaning. The truth is that which endures, has permanence and stability, as opposed to that which is unstable and changeable.

The basic fact of God's relationship to man can be described as a "covenant." God has promised that he will always be the God who reaches out to men to save them from their sinfulness. The truth of the Bible does not depend on whether all its statements and descriptions of everything, of creation, of the details of the Exodus, etc., are a literal account of events as they occurred.

The inquiry must run in another line. The Bible portrays God's faithfulness to his covenant, to his freely-chosen relationship with man. The Bible would be untrue if what is recorded in it about God's fidelity and stability is false. If God had actually abandoned his relationship with his people, if he ceased being the loving, freeing God portrayed in the pages of Scripture, then the Bible lies.

The truth of the Bible rests in its affirmations that God has remained faithful to his promises to love and save men, that he has demonstrated that love and salvation in history, that he continues to love and save in the present and will go on doing so as long as there are men who search for a life they cannot grasp by themselves.

3. The ultimate truth of the Bible is to be found in the

Bible as a whole, as a unity. The truth of any individual passage is relative to the truth of the larger section of which it is part, to the truth of the Book in which it is found, to the truth of Jesus Christ.

Some examples:

The prophets spoke about the wanderings in the "desert." In the desert wanderings after the liberation from Egypt and before the Israelites found a homeland of their own, they were totally at the mercy of wind, sand and storm. Without home, without food, without water, they had to rely totally on God to provide for them. The prophets most often thought of this time as the ideal of God's relation with his people. This total dependence on God is the ideal attitude for life. Hence, the prophets praised the desert as a symbol of the correct stance of man toward God.

On the other hand, the first Books of the Bible often portray the time in the desert as a time when the people grumble and complain about their hard life. They lapse into rebellion against God.

Obviously these pictures cannot be reconciled. Yet each in its own way in its own context has its element of truth.

In Matthew 6.4, Jesus says, "Keep your deeds of mercy secret and your Father who sees in secret will repay you." This sounds like a command to do all good in a way that no one will notice.

But in Matthew 5.16, Jesus had already said, "Your light must shine before men so that they may see goodness in your acts and give praise to your heavenly Father." This seems like the exactly opposite counsel to 6.4.

Only by taking each saying in its context and putting the two together does the complete teaching of Jesus emerge. Men are to do good to lead others to see their loving Father who works in them, but not to build their own reputation.

Much of what the Old Testament teaches was reinterpreted by Jesus or the early Church. The dietary and social regulations which fill so many pages of the first five Books of the Old Testament lose their importance for Christians. They were true as part of a process, a time-conditioned expression of the mutual ties between God and man. With the coming of Jesus their significance was taken up in something greater.

This does not downplay the value of the Old Testament but places it in perspective as part of a journey leading to Jesus.

Human experience offers a parallel. A child has an unformed understanding of God. That understanding is affected for better or worse by what happens in the child's life. Through the example of his parents and people around him, his own experiences, the instruction he receives, God becomes for him more or less real and important in his life. When things go well, the man grown from this child should have a more mature, a deeper relationship to God as a result of his reflection on all he has seen of himself, of life, of God working in life.

So, too God's revelation of himself is a process. The community, moved and led by individuals within it, reflected on what God had done in the past, on the realities of its own situation in the light of faith, and came to a growing appreciation of God's dealings. At the culmination of the process came the life and teaching of Jesus.

The problem of evil is another case in point. The historical work made up of the Books of Joshua, Judges, 1-2 Samuel, 1-2 Kings has a simple and straightforward answer for the problem of evil. When they are faithful to God, the people are rewarded with long life, material prosperity, victory over their enemies, etc. If they suffer, if there is drought, hunger, defeat in war, it is because they have sinned against God.

The Book of Job moves beyond this answer. When Job's world crumbles around him — his family dead, his health and wealth gone — he looks to his friends for some explanation.

They mouth the traditional solution. "Job, this is happening because you have done something wrong. Repent. Tell God you are sorry and beg his pardon. Then he will deal with you more kindly."

Job will have none of this. He says, "I have not done wrong. I have not brought these evils on myself by sin. Why am I suffering? "

The final answer in the Book of Job is God's challenge to him to ponder the mysteries as well as the order and purpose in nature. Job must trust that God can bring meaning out of his suffering just as the Lord brings meaning out of the operations of nature.

The Book of Wisdom takes this still further. To the difficult question "If God is good and just, why do good people so often suffer? " Wisdom responds, "There is another life beyond this one in which all real and apparent injustices are put right."

This developing insight into the problem of evil leads to the teachings of Jesus. They are true as part of a process which culminates in him. To stop anywhere along the line is to stop short.

At the same time, it would be a great misunderstanding and impoverishment of Scripture to extract only what Jesus said and ignore all that went before which leads up to what he had to say and the way he said it.

APPLYING THE PRINCIPLES

To determine the truth of a biblical passage, the following are key considerations:

1. *What is the author's intention?*

In the Gospel story of the curing of the blind man/men by Jesus going in/out of Jericho, where exactly do the individual authors intend to place the weight of their teaching? Not very likely on the details, except as these contribute to the teaching about Jesus.

Before one can accuse the Bible of error, there must be a serious and scholarly effort to determine as precisely as possible what the author really meant to teach in a particular passage.

In the story of creation in Genesis 1-3, was the main concern of the people who created, preserved, transmitted and put in final form these chapters to hand on for all men scientific information about the origins of the world? If it was, this concern is strangely out of joint with the rest of the Bible.

2. *With what qualification is a point made?*

Is an insight or teaching presented as certainly true? as possible? as doubtful? as a passing remark?

If you were asked how many people there are in your town, you might answer, "15,000." For your questioner to respond immediately from his census statistics, "Ha! You're lying! There are 12,272," would be foolishness. It is quite likely that you do not know the exact number. But since you have lived in the town for twenty years and are very familiar with it, you make an educated guess. Very likely you had no intention of giving an exact number, only an approximate one which, however, is close enough to the real situation to convey a substantially true picture. Of course, if you meant to make a definite claim that there are exactly 15,000 people, no more, no less, you would be wrong.

This also holds true for the Bible. Before the authors can be accused of error, or mistakes, or lying, there must be dialogue with them to try to determine just how much they are willing to sink or swim with a statement. This is especially true when the biblical author is using other sources from which he is copying. Does he intend to make all that is said in these sources his own? Or does he simply pass on what his sources made available to him without passing judgment on it except to find it useful in his overall plan?

Paul's letter to Titus has a passage which is a classical example of this situation. Paul quotes a current proverb about the people with whom Titus had to work. "Cretans have ever been liars, beasts, and lazy gluttons." Paul adds, "and that is the simple truth" (Tit 2.12).

Does this mean that a part of God's message for all mankind forever is that Cretans are liars? Or is it simply the tempermental explosion from a man frustrated by problems his young protégé is facing in trying to keep order and peace in a difficult community on the island of Crete?

Would you be willing to go to your death holding to the eternal, literal validity of "Every cloud has a silver lining"?

3. *What literary forms are involved?*

Vatican II *(Dogmatic Constitution on Divine Revelation,* n. 12) states, "Truth is proposed and expressed in a variety of ways, depending on whether a text is history of one kind or another, or whether its form is that of prophecy, poetry, or some other type of speech. The interpreter must investigate what meaning the sacred writer intended to express and actually expressed in particular circumstances as he used contemporary literary forms in accordance with the situation of his own time and culture. For the correct understanding of what the sacred writer wanted to assert, due attention must be paid to the customary and characteristic styles of perceiving, speaking, and narrating which prevailed at the time of the sacred writers and to the customs men normally followed at that period in their everyday dealings with one another."

Literary forms are not mysterious phantoms that should throw us into panic. We use them every day. They are simply the various ways we use to communicate with one another.

The communicated word may be spoken.

One Sunday morning, Mr. and Mrs. Smith watch the television *news report.* Then, at church, they hear a *sermon.* Back home at dinner, one of their guests tells a *joke.* When Mrs. Smith invites her guests to go into the living room while she does the cleaning up, they reply, "Many hands make light work," a *proverb.* Later in the afternoon, they listen to an *interview* on the radio and fill out the day by going to a *lecture* in the evening.

Each of these ways of communicating has its own rules, its own peculiar ways to make points, to tell the truth, to get ideas across.

When the communicated word is written rather than spoken, a similar variety is possible.

On a rainy evening, Mrs. Smith writes a *letter* to a friend in Europe. Mr. Smith pores over the *report* he must make on the possibilities of expansion for his company. Their son in college struggles over a *term paper* for his history course, while their teen-age daughter puts together a *book report* for her English class. Their youngest child bites the eraser on his pencil while planning the *poem* he has to compose for his next day in school. Finally, their work done, they relax. Mr. Smith opens his copy of the latest best-selling *novel;* Mrs. Smith picks up her *Time,* a *magazine,* while Junior goes back to his *comic book.*

Again, the possibility of writing in different styles to accomplish different purposes is almost unlimited. All these diverse ways of writing are *literary forms.* Literary forms are the stuff of human communication and it should come as no surprise that they are the material out of which the Bible is constructed. This is simply acknowledging that the Bible is the word of God in the words of men. No form, no style of legitimate human expression is unworthy of being used by God to reveal himself to men.

Some are uneasy about literary forms in the Bible because they sense a denial of the historical character of the Scriptures. This is a danger only on the assumption that everything in the Bible is meant as strict literal history. It is not. No more than every statement of ours conveys strict, literal history, as, for example, "It rained cats and dogs this morning." Properly understood, the determination and recognition of literary forms aids in establishing the truth of the Bible because only by applying knowledge of literary forms does what the author wanted to say come through clearly.

The truth of the *parable* of the Good Samaritan or the Prodigal Son is not in the fact that there ever was such a good Samaritan, or such a wayward boy and his father, but in the lesson of God's love which Jesus teaches by using a pedagogical method, the parable form, popular with the rabbis of his day.

If the account of Jonah and the large fish was intended from the very beginning by its author as a teaching story and not as factual narrative, to take it as a literal description of a series of events is to misread it, to make it say something the author never wanted to say.

The proper attitude for beginning is an open mind. What do the data indicate? They rather strongly indicate that the Jonah story is a story and not a day-by-day chronicle. This does not destroy its value but helps us to appreciate its value more. We understand that the real historical character of the work is the lesson being taught and not the story framework that conveys the lesson.

The story of Jonah, as a protest against a narrow view of God's love as confined to a special group of people but as an affirmation of God's love for all men, is a high point in the Old Testament. How many readers are aware of that? How many have gotten side-tracked by puzzlement about the size of the fish, about a man surviving in the belly of a fish, etc.?

Scripture is filled with literary forms; epic poetry, love poetry, hymns, legends, parables, allegories, proverbs, sermons, history.

The task of the interpreter and teacher is to determine the literary form so that he might ascertain in what way the truth about God and men is to be found in each particular passage.

4. What kind of science is in the Bible?

The problem of the truth of so-called "scientific" statements in the Bible is generally solved by determining the formal object—what the author really means—and by an awareness that the science in the Bible is science "according to appearances," as was explained previously. Since the Bible is not intended as a science text-book, its truth on a scientific level is not guaranteed. In the passages where a "scientific" position emerges, the pertinent question still remains, "What does this say about God and his saving relationship to men? "

Attempts to reconcile the account of creation in seven days with evolutionary theories or the scientific evidence for the millions of years that went into the formation of the universe are misguided. The lesson in the creation story is not scientific but religious, about the ultimate origin and dependence of all things on God. Creation, for the believer, is more than a scientific issue. It is a religious truth. It is concerned not only with how things began but also with God's continuing relationship with the world. His creative power is directed to bringing all men to love him, and so to live in peace and harmony with one another and with all creation. This is something infinitely more profound and significant than the scientific questions about the details of beginnings, as valid as they might be. The impact of God's involvement with creation does not depend on what science may or may not discover about evolution or any other scientific theory.

5. What kind of history is in the Bible?

The problem here is not so simply solved. We cannot simply hold, "It makes no difference whether or not there is anything historically true in the Bible. The important thing is the theological lesson."

Christianity claims to be based on certain events: among them, the Exodus from Egypt, the life and teachings, death and resurrection of Jesus Christ. If all these are merely "stories," then what we hold as fundamental—that God acts in history—is a lie. We have been trapped in a pathetic hoax. To put it another way, God's saving history with men presupposes the historical truth of certain key events.

But in searching for this historical truth, we must be aware that the historical writing of the Bible, and indeed of ancient literature in general, is different from ours. It is not the listing of facts with all the data that might substantiate them, the documents and journals that verify them, the sworn testimony of witnesses. It is not the important figure caught forever on video tape, speaking the actual words on the actual occasion.

Biblical history is history interpreted, history with meanings and theological insights already woven in.

In the account of the Exodus from Egypt as found now in the Book of Exodus, indications are that there are at least three different versions worked together, the latest of which is about 600 years later than the earliest. Each version presents the story of the deliverance of the Israelites from Egypt in its own way. Each adds its own insights and interpretaions. The resulting narrative in the Book of Exodus is thus a very complex piece of work.

Try to imagine how the story of the Revolutionary War battles of Lexington and Concord would sound if composed under these conditions.

A few months after the battle in 1775, some of the Massachusetts farmers who fought in it remember the shouts of their fellow militiamen when the British started to retreat. They take a boastful slogan, "We clouted them back to Britain" (purely imaginative), and make it the theme of a patriotic song which elaborates on the victory.

Some years later, in 1825 to pick a date, an old man who had been at the battle as a youth puts down some of his reminiscences of Lexington and Concord. By now, the memory of the event has faded. He is open to the dreams and imaginings that come from knowing that one has taken part in an event that shaped history. His story of the battle grows. Details are filled in. Later understanding is laid over the simple account of the battle. Accuracy suffers, but the substantial truth remains intact.

A century later, in 1941, America is about to be swallowed into the Second World War. Still another writer decides to prepare a screenplay for a movie about Lexington and Concord. He is concerned with more than the historical facts. Hoping to fire American patriotism, he very deliberately chooses what he will say about the battle and how he will say it. Using the events of the battle as a framework, he stresses the bravery of the colonials in the face of the foreign oppressors. Perhaps he plays on the tyranny and cruelty of the British soldiers. Instances of bravery among the hastily summoned farmers are filled out with details, some of them imaginary.

Finally, in 1975, a collector of American traditions takes these three very different accounts of the battle, none of which is naked history, and stirs them into a more or less lumpy porridge.

If you can imagine this process, and see how far it would be from a bare recital of facts, names and dates, you can begin to appreciate the kind of history that much of the Bible is.

In this kind of "history," a blow-by-blow account of the battle would be out of the question. However, there would be no doubt about the importance of the battle. In fact, that the battle was fought and that it was significant would be emphasized by the recurrence of the memory of it over two centuries.

Likewise, the discovery of at least three variations of the story of liberation from Egypt, with 600 years separating the earliest from the latest, does not deny the truth of liberation from slavery in Egypt. On the contrary, the story of the liberation must have been very basic in the life of the people. After all, they preserved it and passed it on from generation to generation over six centuries.

However, the knowledge that we have now one story woven from three cautions us to step carefully in trying to reconstruct in all details the events of the Exodus.

Another example from the New Testament: the accounts of the passion and death of Jesus in the Gospels.

These, too, are written with theological aspects in mind. Legitimate questions can be raised about whether some of the details in the narrative of the death of Jesus are literal descriptions of events or whether they are meant to suggest certain biblical themes and their fulfillment in Jesus.

Matthew 27 relates that when Jesus was crucified, "From

noon onward, there was darkness over the whole land until midafternoon. . .the earth quaked, boulders split . . ." Without denying out of hand that such events may have actually happened through the intervention of God, there is room for inquiring whether these marvelous upheavals hint at more than literal description.

Darkness, earthquakes, cosmic turmoil, are familiar poetic images in the Old Testament for the Day of Yahweh, the moment of God's (final) intervention in the world to destroy the forces of evil and establish his own saving rule. By describing such events as taking place at the death of Jesus, the Gospel writers may not mean to describe physical events at all, but to point to the significance of Jesus' death in symbolic language. The death of Jesus on the cross is the day of Yahweh, the unique and final saving act of God which overthrows a world of sin and replaces it with a world ruled by God's love.

Matthew also relates that "the curtain of the sanctuary was torn in two from top to bottom." This curtain hung in the Jewish Temple to separate its interior into a larger room and a smaller one, the smaller being the more sacred and entered only once a year by the High Priest. Rather than describing an actual splitting of the veil, Matthew may be interpreting the death of Jesus by using a symbol. The death of Jesus is to be understood as a "tearing of the curtain," as an end to the system of Jewish worship, as the beginning of a universal religion in which God and salvation will be accessible to all men through Jesus.

Notice that these interpretations in no way deny the historical reality of Jesus' death on the cross. Some details included by the Evangelists were very likely intended to carry an interpretation of that death rather than to give the vivid details that a television reporter might be interested in and would lose his job for not getting.

"Therefore, since everything asserted by the inspired authors or sacred writers must be held to be asserted by the Holy Spirit, it follows that the books of Scripture must be acknowledged as teaching firmly, faithfully, and without error that truth which God wanted to put into the sacred writings for the sake of our salvation." Vatican II: *Dogmatic Constitution on Divine Revelation, n. 11.*

The Bible is not simply a book of historical and scientific facts. It is a book of truth which goes far beyond history or science. The truth has to do with man and God and their relations with each other and the meaning of life.

Sometimes this truth is communicated in accounts of historical events, some of which are fairly accurate reports, while others are elaborate theological constructions. Sometimes this truth is communicated in and through statements about "science." The science is very primitive, often mistaken, but the theological insight is valid none the less. Sometimes the truth is communicated in and through proverbs, love poems, folk stories about local heroes, hymns, popular songs, legends, etc.

Very often the truth communicated is far from being "information" about God. The sermon at a revival meeting, or parish mission is not primarily for "information" but for turning the hearts and minds of men to God, for moving them to recognize their need for God. The words of the prophets are not simply "information." They are the interpretation of life, the call to turn in trust and fidelity to God.

SUGGESTIONS FOR REFLECTION

1. The Church has always believed *that* the Bible is true, but it has grown to a deeper understanding of *how* the Bible is true. After reading this chapter, give one example

of something in the Bible which we understand differently today than we did twenty years ago.

2. At times, there are contradictions and inconsistencies in the Scriptural writings. At other times, the scientific knowledge expressed is erroneous by modern standards. At still other times, history seems to be out of order or mistaken. Knowing this, how can we still say the Bible is true? Use the three ways described in this chapter to show that truth is present through all the Scriptures.

3. Describe some situations in your lifetime when you have come to ever deepening insights into meanings or understanding of truth as you became more mature (e. g. insights into suffering, into the meaning of experience, into the meaning of relationships, into the meaning of life and death).

4. Sometimes prayer groups have trouble with literal meanings of passages in the Scriptures.

What are five principles that could help them determine the interpretation of a particular biblical passage?

5. After reading this chapter, how would you answer a friend from your old school days who asks you angrily, "Why did they lie to us and teach us in school that Adam and Eve ate an apple, that Jonah was swallowed by a whale, that the Red Sea opened up to let the Israelites pass through and then rushed back to drown the Egyptians? "

6. After reading this chapter, how would you answer a Catholic neighbor at a P. T. A. meeting who sees Genesis as being denied, and his religion as being attacked when books and teachers include evolution in the science curriculum?

7. If you were teaching religion, what reason would you give to parents for taking the stories of creation, Adam and Eve and Noah out of the primary books and postponing

them till the intermediate grades or junior high?

8. As a parent, how would you respond to your teenager who comes home from school and, convinced that he is stumping you, says, "The Bible is not history," or "The New Testament is not a biography of Jesus."

CHAPTER IV

THE MAKING OF THE BIBLE

THE BOOKS OF THE BIBLE

THE OLD TESTAMENT*

A. The Pentateuch (i. e. "five volumes")
1. Genesis (Gn)
2. Exodus (Ex)
3. Leviticus (Lv)
4. Numbers (Nm)
5. Deuteronomy (Dt)

B. The "Historical" Books
6. Joshua (Jos)
7. Judges (Jgs)
8. Ruth (Ru)
9. 1 Samuel (1 Sm)
10. 2 Samuel (2 Sm)
11. 1 Kings (1 Kgs)
12. 2 Kings (2 Kgs)
13. 1 Chronicles (1 Chr)
14. 2 Chronicles (2 Chr)
15. Ezra (Ezr)
16. Nehemiah (Neh)
17. Tobit (Tb)
18. Judith (Jdt)
19. Esther (Est)
20. 1 Maccabees (1 Mc)
21. 2 Maccabees (2 Mc)

C. The Wisdom Books
22. Job (Jb)

*There are other divisions possible.

60

23. Psalms (Ps)
24. Proverbs (Prv)
25. Ecclesiastes (or Qoheleth) (Eccl)
26. Song of Songs (Sg)
27. Wisdom (Wis)
28. Sirach (or Ecclesiasticus) (Sir)

D. The Prophetical Books
29. Isaiah (Is)
30. Jeremiah (Jer)
31. Lamentations (Lam)
32. Baruch (Bar)
33. Ezekiel (Ez)
34. Daniel (Dn)
35. Hosea (Hos)
36. Joel (Jl)
37. Amos (Am)
38. Obadiah (Ob)
39. Jonah (Jon)
40. Micah (Mi)
41. Nahum (Na)
42. Habakkuk (Hb)
43. Zephaniah (Zep)
44. Haggai (Hg)
45. Zechariah (Zec)
46. Malachi (Mal)

THE NEW TESTAMENT

A. The Gospels
1. Matthew (Mt)
2. Mark (Mk)
3. Luke (Lk)
4. John (Jn)

B. 5. Acts of the Apostles (Acts)

C. The Pauline Literature
6. The Letter to the Romans (Rom)
7. The First Letter to the Corinthians (1 Cor)

8. The Second Letter to the Corinthians (2 Cor)
9. The Letter to the Galatians (Gal)
10. The Letter to the Ephesians (Eph)
11. The Letter to the Philippians (Phil)
12. The Letter to the Colossians (Col)
13. The First Letter to the Thessalonians (1 Thes)
14. The Second Letter to the Thessalonians (2 Thes)
15. The First Letter to Timothy (1 Tm)
16. The Second Letter to Timothy (2 Tm)
17. The Letter to Titus (Ti)
18. The Letter to Philemon (Phlm)
19. The Letter to the Hebrews (Heb)

D. The "Catholic" Letters
20. The Letter of James (Jas)
21. The First Letter of Peter (1 Pt)
22. The Second Letter of Peter (2 Pt)
23. The First Letter of John (1 Jn)
24. The Second Letter of John (2 Jn)
25. The Third Letter of John (3 Jn)
26. The Letter of Jude (Jude)
27. Revelation (also called Apocalypse) (Rv)

E. 27. Revelation (also called Apocalypse) (Rv)

What makes these books *the* Bible? Of the countless works written before these books, contemporaneous with them, after them, how did these get to be recognized as special, as inspired by God in a way that no other works ever have been? How do we know that of all the books which have provided profound insights into the meaning of life and have influenced the movements of mankind that this list of books is uniquely the work of God and man? How do we know we are backing the right side by putting so much stock in this little collection out of all the literary output of human history?

To begin to work toward an answer to these questions, a division into two lines of inquiry is necessary. One is historical. "Can we trace how these books, the Bible, got

worked into a special category?   What transpired that ended
with these books being called 'inspired by God' "?
The other is theological. "On what grounds did our pre-
decessors determine that the Bible is from God?   On what
grounds do men today make such a decision? "

A technical word must be introduced here. The word,
"canon," comes from a Greek word meaning "rule,"
"standard," "measure." As applied to the Bible, "canon"
refers to those books which are recognized as being inspired
by God, as being parts of the Bible. A book is "canonical"
if it truly belongs to that group of books accepted as inspired by God.

THE CANON OF THE OLD TESTAMENT

THE HEBREW CANON OF THE OLD TESTAMENT
(THE HEBREW SCRIPTURES)

As we have already seen, the formation of the individual
Books of the Old Testament was a complicated process.
The process of collecting these individual books into what
Christians call the "Old Testament" was just as intricate.
To go into all the details would probably be telling more
about the canon than most people want to know. Some
highlights and examples will suffice.

Each Book of the Old Testament has its own story. Fre-
quently this story begins with small pieces of tradition
passed on by word of mouth, moves to putting some of these
traditions together (still in memory and passed on by telling), moves still further to actual writing, to building on,
editing and adding onto this first written material. Finally,
often in the course of several centuries, a Book reached its
present form.

Eventually the people of Israel gathered these individual
Books into larger units that go by the names of Torah, the
Prophets, the Writings.

The *Torah* is the first five Books of the Bible: Genesis, Exodus, Leviticus, Numbers and Deuteronomy. Often translated as "law," Torah is more accurately "teaching" or "instruction." This section of the Scriptures contains, along with the creation story, the traditions about Israel's early days: the life and times of its ancestors, Abraham, Isaac, Jacob, Joseph; the slave years in Egypt and God's deliverance from that slavery; the years spent homeless in the barren wilderness; the wonder of God's special relationship with Israel formulated at Sinai, a mountain in the desert. The Torah includes the great mass of laws that spell out Israel's part in this relationship with God. It ends with the people poised and ready to enter the Promised Land.

How did the Torah grow? Through the living faith of Israel! The first experiences of liberation from slavery, of the awareness of a unique relationship between God and this people, had to be kept alive and deepened. This happened chiefly in the context of worship carried on at sanctuaries where Yahweh, the God of Israel, was honored. Part of the religious ceremonial involved the recitation of creeds, of summaries of the main elements of the common faith. We Catholics still recite a 1500 year-old creed at our liturgy on Sundays and great feasts.

Deuteronomy 26.5-9 is a creed, an expression of faith, to be recited by the Israelite at the sanctuary. In speaking of his ancestor, Jacob, he professes:"My father was a wandering Aramean who went down to Egypt with a small household and lived there as an alien. But there he became a nation great, strong and numerous. When the Egyptians maltreated and oppressed us, imposing hard labor upon us, we cried to the Lord, the God of our fathers, and he heard our cry and saw our affliction, our toil and our oppression. He brought us out of Egypt with his strong hand and out streched arm, with terrifying power, with signs and wonders; and bringing us into this country, he gave us this land flowing with milk and honey."

Notice the main articles of the creed; life in Egypt, oppression there, deliverance from slavery, the promise of a land.

In the recent past in the Catholic Church, one pattern of preaching revolved around analyzing the Apostles' Creed, article by article. A number of Sundays were devoted to bringing out the meaning and implications of each statement of the Creed. The preacher could spend weeks explaining, "I believe in God, the Father Almighty," or "Creator of heaven and earth."

So too, Israel's faith centered around creeds, around expressions of belief in what God had done for it in history. The first five Books of the Bible elaborate on, illustrate, fill out, the articles of the creed with the traditions formed by the life and history of the people.

The laws express in human terms what response God expected in return for what he did for his people. These laws were preserved at the shrines to which the people went to worship Yahweh. They inquired of priest and prophet what their relationship to God implied for daily life. The response was a living code of law which was constantly being reinterpreted as times and situations changed.

We have been living through a similar process. To be a Christian in the atomic and jet age, with the population explosion, with pollution of land, water and air, with science and technology riding high, makes demands that are different from those made on a Christian of three hundred years ago. Then life was lived mainly on farms and in small villages. Our highly complex society with its peculiar problems had not yet been born.

Likewise, it was one thing for an Israelite to be a nomad wandering in the desert. Being related to Yahweh, the God of Israel, carried certain responsibilities and a way of fidelity that had to be spelled out to deal with circumstances likely to be met in that manner of life.

When Israel settled down to become a nation of small farmers and tradesmen, surrounded by a culture more advanced than its own, in close contact with religious practices and beliefs different from those of its past, the understanding of the relationship with Yahweh had to be reinterpreted.

The old explanations and guidelines were associated with a style of life that no longer existed. The truth of God's loving and caring for his people had not changed, but now the people had to grapple with what it meant for them to respond to God, to remain faithful to him in a new and very different set of circumstances. Again, much of this re-education took place at the religious shrines of the Israelites where their priests (when everything was working as it should) taught them the implications of their religious ritual for their new life.

Probably the heaviest and steadiest pressure to gather all these traditions into some kind of permanent collection came during the Exile. The Kingdom of Judah had been conquered by the Babylonians in 587 B. C. Its capital city, Jerusalem, had been destroyed; its king, carried off into exile along with a large number of its leaders and educated population. The Temple, the symbol of God's presence among his people, had been reduced to rubble.

By all expectations, the religion of the people of Judah should have died. Everything that stood for the presence of its God — the Promised Land, the holy city, the Temple, the king chosen by God, — had disappeared. The signs of the power and care of God were lost in destruction, death and tears.

But the religion of Israel did not die. It lived on because there were those living as exiles whose clear vision saw that God is greater than any of the signs of his presence.

During the exile, these fierce believers gathered the traditions of the people in whatever form these already existed. Retelling, re-reading, contemplating these traditions and laws which expressed the bond between God and his people would keep the people together. God had not and never would abandon those he loved, if they loved and were faithful to him.

During the Exile, the Torah takes substantially the form that it has today.

A similar outline of development could be sketched for the other parts of the Hebrew Scriptures. However, the point has already been made, and we shall be satisfied with summarizing the conclusions of recent scholarship about the formation of the Hebrew Scriptures as a collection having a special authority from God in so far as this collection was accepted and recognized by the *Jewish community.*

Indications are that by the end of the second century before Christ the Jewish community had a collection of five Books called the *Torah,* to which nothing more was being added or from which nothing was being taken away, and another completed collection of the *Prophets* (which would include most of what our list calls "Historical Books").

There was a third collection that went by the name of *Writings* which was still in a state of flux. No final decision had been made about a relatively large number of works which were considered significant and religiously beneficial for the Jewish community. Were these works also divinely inspired? The answer would come only after the life-style and religious attitudes of the people could insure firm and fixed decisions about the matter.

The pressures of world events again forced the Jews into situations in which a final definition of their sacred books became imperative.

The Exile was not the only identity-shattering experience for the Jews.

From the fifth century B. C. onward, Jews found themselves
scattered all over the Mediterranean world. This is called
the period of dispersion—the Diaspora. In lands not their
own, deliberate attempts were made to turn them from
their faith, often by persecution. An even more persistent
threat came from the erosion that is inevitable when what
seem to be more "enlightened," more "with-it" cultures
meet long-lived "traditions." Men are caught between the
legitimate advances of the here-and-now and their past. They
need ways of holding on to the richness of their past. They
have to have guidelines to know what to accept in man's
development, to recognize what to reject as inauthentic.

The heart of Jewish religious life during this period was the
synagogue, and the heart of the synagogue was the written
Jewish traditions which were read, contemplated, explained,
prayed. These traditions were once again undergoing a reinterpretation to fit the new circumstances of Jewish life.
The interpreters this time were the "men of the Book,"
the Scribes.

What's more, the Jews in the first century of our era found
themselves in a curious situation. A splinter group of Jews,
using the Jewish Scriptures and traditions, had moved off
in its own disturbing direction. This sect was claiming that
God had acted in their time in a unique and definitive way.

In discussions and disputes, these schismatics — eventually
called "Christians" — were actually interpreting the Jewish
Scriptures as leading up to and being fulfilled in Jesus,
called the Christ or the Messiah.

If these "Christians" were going to be accepted or rejected
by the Jewish community, it became imperative to define
the Books which were the legitimate word of God for the
Jewish communities. The word of God was the touchstone
which would determine who were authentic followers of
God, and who were intruders in the community.

After another destruction of Jerusalem, in 70 A. D. by the Romans, surviving Jewish scholars collected around a town named Jamnia, west of Jerusalem by the Mediterranean coast. There, in a manner not yet clear, (we do not know whether there was some formal decree or whether the rabbis simply agreed on what books to accept and which to leave out), the canon of Jewish Scripture took its final shape.

Thus, by the end of the first century A. D., the Jews had fixed for once and for all which books were their sacred books, which books were the written word of God to the exclusion of all others, no matter how edifying or pious these might be.

Please note how far this all is from some ready-made collection handed down very straightforwardly by God in pre-packaged form.

THE CHRISTIAN CANON OF THE OLD TESTAMENT

Notice also that we have been talking about the Jewish people and the turns in history by which they arrived at their collection of inspired books. But what about the Christians? How did they arrive at a collection of sacred books, to a great extent paralleling the Hebrew Scriptures, which they would eventually designate as the "Old Testament"?

Once again, there is a historical process to be traced.

Jesus and the first Christians were Jews. Their sacred Books, their Scriptures, were the same as those of their Jewish contemporaries. They revered the Torah, the Prophets, and a still not defined collection of holy works called "Writings." These were the Scriptures from which Jesus and the apostles and disciples preached. In the New Testament, there are about 350 quotations from these Scriptures and numerous allusions to them.

But the Christians also had to make their own decisions about which Books reflected their past as God's chosen people. If the Jews did not finally decide which Books made up the special category called "Writings" until the end of the first century, then the Christians did not simply inherit from the Jews a ready-made collection they could call the "Old Testament."

Christians were pressed by circumstances to become specific and definite about which Books held special value for them as being God's Books. They disputed and discussed with Jews. These Christians were working out their understanding of Jesus, of themselves, in terms of the Scriptures of the past. They had to know clearly, if they were to continue as a living community, which Books truly constituted their past history and tradition.

By the end of the second century A. D., references in Christian writers indicate that the various Christian communities were generally using the same set of Books, not only those of the Torah and Prophets, but also those of the section known as Writings.

The notable exception was a special group of Books that Catholics call "deutero-canonical" and Protestants call "apocryphal."

The word, "deutero-canonical," comes from Greek and would translate literally as "second canon." However, this translation would be misleading. What the term means to communicate is that these books were defined as belonging to the canon later than the rest of the accepted books. The word, "apocrypha," also from Greek, means "hidden away." Originally it referred to material which was hidden away because it was too mysterious or too profound, or because it was considered heretical.

The name, "deutero-canonical," is given by Catholics to the following Old Testament material:

the Book of Tobit
the Book of Judith
the Book of Wisdom
the Book of Sirach (or Ecclesiasticus)
the First Book of Maccabees
the Second Book of Maccabees
the Book of Baruch
the Book of Daniel: Ch. 3. 24-90; Chs. 13-14
the Book of Esther (parts)

Questions arose about these Books or parts of Books because they were not found in the accepted Hebrew Bible.
For Christians, the issue of the canon narrows to whether
or not these works ought to be recognized as inspired.
Generally, the Church in the West — Rome, North Africa,
Gaul — accepted these books as inspired. By the end of the
fourth century, this acceptance was officially decreed in
statements coming from Church Councils.

The Church in the East moved more slowly and did not
arrive at official acceptance until the end of the seventh
century.

Today Catholics consider the so-called "deutero-canonical"
books as inspired and of the same inspired quality as the
rest of the Old Testament. Protestants generally do not
put these books into their Bibles, or if they do, they include
them in a special section under the heading, "Apocrypha."

THE CANON OF THE NEW TESTAMENT

"It is common knowledge that among all the Scriptures,
even those of the New Testament, the Gospels have a special
pre-eminence, and rightly so, for they are the principal witness
of the life and teaching of the incarnate Word, our Savior.
The Church has always and everywhere held and continues
to hold that the four Gospels are of apostolic origin. For
what the apostles preached in fulfillment of the commission
of Christ, afterwards they themselves and apostolic men,

under the inspiration of the divine Spirit, handed on to us
in writing: the foundation of faith, namely, the fourfold
Gospel, according to Matthew, Mark, Luke, and John.

"Holy Mother Church has firmly and with absolute constancy
held, and continues to hold, that the four Gospels just named,
whose historical character the Church unhesitatingly asserts,
faithfully hand on what Jesus Christ, while living among men,
really did and taught for their eternal salvation until the day
He was taken up into heaven (see Acts 1:1-2). Indeed,
after the ascension of the Lord the apostles handed on to
their hearers what He had said and done. This they did with
that clearer understanding which they enjoyed after they had
been instructed by the events of Christ's risen life and taught
by the light of the Spirit of truth. The sacred authors wrote
the four Gospels, selecting some things from the many which
had been handed on by word of mouth or in writing, reducing
some of them to a synthesis, explicating some things in view
of the situation of their churches, and preserving the form
of proclamation but always in such fashion that they told
us the honest truth about Jesus. For their intention in
writing was that either from their own memory and recol-
lections, or from the witness of those who themselves 'from
the beginning were eyewitnesses and ministers of the word'
we might know 'the truth' concerning those matters about
which we have been instructed (cf. Lk 1:2-4)." *Vatican II:
Dogmatic Constitution on Divine Revelation* nn. 18-19.

The earliest teaching and preaching of the Christians was
carried out by those who were the official "rememberers"
of the community. At first, writing was not involved. Those
who had been close to Jesus, who had been witnesses of
his life and teaching and who had experienced the truth of
the resurrection, were the privileged communicators of the
message and mission of Jesus by word of mouth.

As time passed, two things happened.

Some of the early Christians were overly enthusiastic

about the end of the world. Jesus had promised that
he would return in power and glory to write "finis" to a
sinful world and bring all things under the loving rule of
a good Father. Some expected this to happen soon.

But day followed day and still there was no sign that
tomorrow would not dawn just as today had. And as the
days marched on, death shrank the circle of those who
had known Jesus and his first followers. Now it became
crucial to preserve in an authoritative way the faith of that
privileged community that had known the Lord in his lifetime and in the days after the resurrection.

This need gave birth to the Gospels.

THE GOSPELS

The presidential life of John F. Kennedy spanned roughly
1000 days.

The public life of Jesus of Nazareth filled what was probably an equal or even shorter period of time around the year
30. There are no indications that anything about these days
was written during his lifetime. His friends were both inspired and puzzled by this man who had touched their lives.

After the death of Jesus, these friends, through the resurrection and the coming of the Spirit, saw Jesus and his
work and words in a way that was not possible during his
life-time. They confronted people with the challenge of
Jesus. Both Jews and non-Jews were to find the meaning
of life in what Jesus had done. They announced to the
world around them a basic message: "Jesus has died. Jesus
has risen from the dead. Turn to him for the meaning of
life! " This elementary challenge goes by the name of proclamation or kerygma.

But when some of their hearers were moved by this call to
turn to God through Jesus, further questions were inevitable.

What did it mean for everyday living to "turn to Jesus"? Did it make any difference how one faced people, the way one carried on his business, the way one lived his family life? Was accepting salvation from ignorance and emptiness through Jesus simply the occasion for an emotional high, or did it go further? Who was the God Jesus claimed to speak for, to be uniquely related to?

The first Christian preachers went back to their memories of what Jesus had taught them through their years with him. He had given directions and principles, or examples from which principles might be drawn.

These they began to gather into collections.

But perhaps "collections" is not quite the right word. It conveys a picture of pads filled with notes taken by diligent searchers after witnesses who might remember Jesus. These collections were generally not written but were remembered and taught and passed on by word of mouth. Some did eventually get written down.

These interpretations of how to live if one had accepted Jesus were not simply a matter of gathering up all that could be remembered about Jesus. The followers of Jesus were soon living in different circumstances than the Galilean fishermen who had first walked with the man from Nazareth. They had no hesitation about taking the principles and ideals of Jesus and applying them to new situations which had not arisen during Jesus' lifetime. And since this kind of procedure was acceptable enough in the historical writing of the time, they had no qualms in attributing these later applications to Jesus himself.

This went on for about thirty years, from about 30 to 60 A. D.

The next period, from about 60 to 100 A. D. is the period of the writing of the Gospels. In the various Christian communities men of faith set about to choose from all the traditions of the community as they were being taught and preached, to put them in an order of their choosing. Much they left out. They interpreted words and deeds by the way they arranged them. They followed their own plan and theological outlook.

The result was the Gospels.

An involved and very human procedure indeed — but no less under the direction of the Holy Spirit for all that. Once the books were written, the next step was their acceptance as something special by the other Christian communities outside those from which the Gospels originated.

Tracing out all the details of this stage in Gospel history is not necessary. Suffice it to say that by the end of the second century — about 100 years after the last Gospel had been written — Christian writers are speaking of four and only four Gospels, those of Matthew, Mark, Luke, and John. These writers represent such geographically widespread areas as Syria, Rome, and what is now France.

A similar history can be sketched for the rest of the Books of the New Testament; the Letters, the Acts of the Apostles, the Apocalypse. By the end of the second century, Christian communities everywhere had the same basic set of writings that were considered definitive and unique.

It is true that there was on-going discussion, at least by some persons and in some localities, about a number of New Testament writings; the Letter to the Hebrews, the Letter of James, the Second Letter of Peter, the Second and Third Letters of John, the Letter of Jude, and the Apocalypse.

The questions about including these Books in the canon were generally settled by the fifth century. The answer was "Yes."

At the same time, some of the early Christian communities

included with their sacred writings works which would later be removed from the inspired collection.

THE CRITERIA FOR ACCEPTING BOOKS
INTO THE CANON

In the historical process of the formation of the canon, is it possible to pinpoint the qualifications that were required for any work to be considered inspired?

The following factors seem to have been significant.

1. *Apostolicity*

The communities accepted writings that went back to the first Christians, to those who had been with Jesus and the disciples taught by them. Origin in this "apostolic generation," which lasted till the end of the first century, gave a work a privileged position over the devotional, theological and moral writings of others who came later in the Church, no matter how profound, moving and good these might be.

2. *Orthodoxy*

Some early works in the form of "gospels" claim to be the production of apostles presenting the life and teachings of Jesus.

In these "gospels," we might read of a young Jesus who fits well the term, "spoiled brat." He strikes dead those who accidentally knock into him. He makes tricks out of miracles, turning little mud figures into birds, and so on.

Other early stories of the apostles which sound much like the canonical Acts of the Apostles relate how sex is evil and how the apostles encouraged all Christians to turn from sex, even to the extent of avoiding marriage.

There are other writings that appear for all the world like the letters in the legitimate New Testament.

Much of this literature lived for a while in the Church or in groups within the Church but was eventually rejected as not being a true expression of its faith in Jesus. For the curious, this material is still available today and is termed "apocryphal" by Catholics and "pseudepigraphical" by Protestants.

3. *Use by the Community*

In the dynamic, Spirit-guided life of the community, certain writings proved their value and power in the practical test of use in teaching and in celebration of the liturgy. Constant and fruitful employment tended to bring certain works to the forefront.

We might conclude, then, that the New Testament consists of those works which the early Christian communities came to recognize as inspired by God because they were of apostolic origin, because they reflected the true faith of the believing community, because the test of use in the community had demonstrated their Spirit-filled character.

THE THEOLOGICAL ISSUE OF THE FORMATION OF THE NEW TESTAMENT

So far, our concern has been with history. In so far as we can reconstruct it, what was the historical process by which the early Christians came to write and gather together the collection of writings now called the New Testament?

There is a further issue:
How can these books that have been accepted as the word of God be legitimated as actually being that; that is, the word of God? Is there any way of proving that these works, which the Church through its life has accepted, are truly from God in a sense so special that all other works exist on a different level?

One can accept any part of the Old or New Testament, and the Old and New Testaments as a whole, as God's word only in faith. There can be no "proof" of divine origin.

Our faith is that the Holy Spirit operated in the early Christian communities by directing them to recognize what really came from him. These writings, as the expression of the light brought and lived by Jesus, remain the standard for all Christians, both as individuals and as a community. To fail to preserve the teachings of the Scriptures, to distort or pervert those teachings, is to lose the claim to truth.

That early period of the life of the Church was different from the life of the Church today.

This does not mean that the Spirit was working then and is not working today, or that God was revealing himself then and is not revealing himself today, or that God was entering into a loving relationship with men then and is not entering into such relationships today. It simply means that in the period in human history in which the Son of God became man to reveal the Father to all men and to bring himself into the most intimate type of relationship possible with men, something unique and unrepeatable was happening. The community of believers of that day and its faith was to serve as the guide for the Church that would continue the life of Jesus in the world. That community formulated and preserved the essential reality about God revealed through Jesus.

There is room for development, for deeper understanding because the reality of God cannot be captured in any set of words conditioned by its own time and culture. There is room for development because as the face of the world changes, it needs to see again what God is all about. Man faced with the hydrogen bomb, with genetic control, with pollution, has different things on his mind than the man of the first century A. D.

The truth revealed by Jesus is open to speak to all situations under the guidance of the Spirit living in and moving the Church.

SUGGESTIONS FOR REFLECTION

1. Try to describe how the creeds, or summaries of the main elements of a common faith, began and developed in ancient Israel.

Why was this important in building a sense of oneness in the People of God? Do the creeds we say today (Nicene, Apostles) bring about the same unifying effect for you? For most Catholics?

2. Israel's "laws expressed in human terms what response God expected in return for what he did for his people . . . The response was a living code of law which was constantly being reinterpreted as times and situations changed."

In your experience, have you ever wished that "times and situations" would not change? That they would change? Some Catholics today do not realize that times and changing situations have also affected the insights into the ten commandments, the creeds, the commandments of the Church, etc. How could they be helped to see and accept the fact that change and reinterpretation enter into everything in life?

3. God expected his code of law to be "living and constantly reinterpreted," to be a living relationship with him as times and situations changed.

What does this mean for daily life in our times with its problems of hunger, world population increase, inflation, the rise in delinquency, energy crises, disregard for human life?

4. The Israelites suffered a real religious crisis when Jerusalem and the Temple were destroyed and when they were scattered into exile. It seemed to them that "everything that stood for the presence of their God" had disappeared. Have you ever felt this way in your life? Do you think some Catholics are today experiencing a similar sense of

spiritual crisis because familiar signs of God's presence seem gone.

5. The Israelites in exile had to come to realize that God is more than any of the signs of his presence. This made those who could accept this truth stronger, more united, more committed to God.
Do we have hints that this may be happening in the Church today?

6. It was often difficult for the Jews to know what of their traditions of the past to hold on to, what of the new ideas of the present to accept.
Have you ever experienced this tension? Is this tension present in the Church today? How did the early Christians coming from Judaism, resolve the problem? How did the other Jews resolve it?

7. What was the role of the community of believers among the Jews and among the early Christians in deciding which Books in their religious heritage were inspired? Did any individuals have especially important roles? How did history have a hand in this process? Do you think it was easier to be a Christian in those days than it is now?

8. Protestants and Jews differ from Catholics in the Books of the Bible that they accept.
How would you explain this to a non-Catholic neighbor? What three qualities were expected for a writing to have "canonical" authority?

9. The early Christian community was different from ours today because life and world outlook were different. Why do we consider its message as still essential for the twentieth century?

10. Both "tradition" and "change" have always been values in Christianity. Can you think of ways both "tradition" and "change" can exist together as values in a family, or in a town, or in a Church?

CHAPTER V

THE TEXT OF THE BIBLE

Bruce Metzger, a respected Biblical scholar, has written about a curiosity in the 1934 edition of *Webster's New International Dictionary of the English Language.*

An entry reads: dord (dôrd), n. Physics & Chem. Density.

For ten years, this entry remained in place in the prestigious dictionary — despite the fact that there is no such word in the English language as "dord." How did it get into the dictionary?

A little detective work traced out the following process.

The correct original entry was:
d. or D., Physics & Chem. Density.
Somehow the periods slipped out leaving:
d or D, Physics & Chem. Density.

Somewhere else along the line of editing and printing after this, the spaces disappeared and "dorD" was born. Obviously this is incorrect, and the most obvious correction that needs to be made is to reduce the final capital "D" to a small "d." And so it happened.

Behold, "dord"! And the peculiar way in which a word that was really not a word made its debut in a famous dictionary. The new combination of letters sprang not only from human errors but from attempts to correct a mistake when recognized.

Even without this example, the situation is a familiar one. Editorial and typographical errors turn up every day in newspapers, magazines, books. *The New Yorker* magazine fills what would otherwise be empty space with examples of such blunders that make for funny reading.

If mistakes can creep into modern writing and copying efforts with all our technology, then we must be warned about the possibilities of changes taking place in the text of the Bible. We do not have the original of any of the Books of the Bible. We have copies of the original.

These copies were made under trying conditions. Men copied by hand either from a manuscript in front of them, or from dictation by a reader. As is the case with us, the eyes of the copyists could misread words. Their eyes could slip from one line to another without their realizing it. They could copy some work or phrase or line twice. They could hear inaccurately what the reader intoned.
Add to this the exhaustion of eyesight and concentration from copying all day, the hazards of poor lighting, etc., and it should come as no shock to learn that many errors (meaning many changes in the original wording) got into the Bible in the course of copying.

To stay with examples from the New Testament, the earliest copies — only parts of them still exist — go back to the second half of the second and the beginning of the third century. This means that our earliest fragmentary copies of the new Testament are a century older than the originals.

The oldest copy of any part of the New Testament known to exist today is a little piece of papyrus with four verses from Chapter 18 of St. John's Gospel. Scholars date this little relic to sometime around the year 150, or somewhat earlier.

The problem simply put is that our earliest texts of the

Gospels are copies of copies. In such a situation, a whole series of miracles would have been required of God to keep word changes out.

And not all changes that take place in a text happen by chance or accident. Sometimes copyists very deliberately make changes in what they are copying thinking to correct mistakes they have found, or believe they have found. "d. or D." would not have turned into "dord" if some proof-readers or editors had not set about to correct what looked like an error to them. If you or I were copying a newspaper story and came across a misspelled word, a very natural urge would be to spell the word correctly in our copy.

Early copyists of the New Testament, besides making accidental changes also made what they thought were corrections.

The differences between one copy of the New Testament and another, which occurred either because of slips in copying or because of deliberate attempts at making the text "better," are called "variants."

One branch of the study of the Bible is called "textual criticism." Textual criticism tries to study all the variants that appear in copies of a given passage and to select the one that would seem to correspond to what the original reading was.

It is a very complex field.

EXAMPLES OF VARIANTS

A few illustrations will serve to highlight what "variants" are and how they happen.

In a vision in the Book of Revelation (6.4), the seer describes a horse by using a Greek word which some manuscripts have as "puros" and others as "purros." Either of these words makes sense, especially in the vivid imagery of the Book of Revelation. "Puros" means "fiery," "purros," "red." There is either "a fiery horse" or "a red horse"

How the two possibilities came into being is easy enough to spot. Either some copyists wrote two "r's" where there was originally only one, or others wrote one "r" where originally there were two. The textual critic has to decide. And decide he has, that "purros" is correct. The horse is "red." We need not go into all the reasons for this choice.

Luke 2.33 has Mary and Joseph with the baby Jesus in the Temple. Some old texts have "The child's father and mother were marveling at what was being said about him."

Other old copies have, "As Joseph and his (i. e., Jesus') mother stood there, . . . "

Which version is correct? Should the text speak about "the child's father" or "Joseph? "

Experts have decided that the correct original reading was "the child's father." A later copyist, afraid that referring to Joseph like this might compromise the belief in the virgin birth of Jesus because it might be interpreted as implying that Joseph was the natural father of the Christ child, changed "his father" to "Joseph."

These two examples illustrate the possibilities and types of changes that took place in the text of the New Testament in the process of copying.

Does this historical reality leave us without a hope of getting back to the text of the New Testament as it was originally written, which is after all what we want?

By comparing all the early copies of the Greek New Testament that are available and studying all the variants in these copies, between 150,000 to 200,000 variations on the approximately 150,000 words of the New Testament emerge. Staggering!

But not really. Most of the variants are insignificant and make little difference for the understanding of the text. Then, by applying the rules that experience has proved to be most useful in reconstructing the original text, 90% of the New Testament text is certainly established. In the remaining 10%, variations of any consequence are few and far between.

The New Testament as it was written is available to us today.

TRANSLATIONS OF THE BIBLE

The Old Testament was originally written in Hebrew, with some small sections in another Semitic language called Aramaic, and a few books in Greek. The New Testament was written in Greek.

Since relatively few readers of the Bible can read these original languages, another step is called for to get the Bible out from the shelf under the coffee table into the hands of anyone interested in it. This further step is translation.

This calls for a few words about some of the most commonly used English translations of the Bible.

The King James or Authorized Version (KJV or AV) was published in 1611, the result of the efforts of English scholars appointed to the task by King James I. Eventually it became the classical non-Catholic Christian Bible, still much in use today and greatly admired for the beauty of its language. If the Bible is being read at a non-Catholic service and the language is ancient-sounding with "thee's" and "thou's" much in evidence, chances are very good that this is the King James.

85

The Revised Standard Version (RSV) New Testament appeared in 1946 and the whole Bible in 1952. Also under non-Catholic auspices, the translators aimed to include in their translation the progress that had been made over the years since the publication of the King James in determining a more accurate text of the Bible. They were also concerned about putting the Scriptures into more modern English.

The Common Bible is the title given to an ecumenical version of the RSV. It contains the Revised Standard text and has the approval of Protestant, Catholic and Greek Orthodox authorities to encourage the reading of the same version of the Scriptures by all Christians.

The New English Bible (NEB) is still another attempt to render the Bible in contemporary English. Translated by a committee representing the major non-Roman Catholic religious bodies in Great Britain, the New Testament appeared in 1961 and the Old Testament in 1970.

The *Good News Bible* or *Today's English Version* (TEV) New Testament was first published in 1966 by the American Bible Society as *Good News for Modern Man*. The popular complete Bible appeared in 1976. It is intended for "people who speak English as their mother tongue. . . As a distinctly new translation, it does not conform to traditional vocabulary or style, but seeks to express the meaning of the Greek text in words and forms accepted by people everywhere who employ English as a means of communication."

The Jerusalem Bible (JBE) a Catholic translation, appeared in 1966, the work of English scholars. This version is made from the original languages but uses the notes and translation into French prepared by scholars centered in Jerusalem. It is very appealing from the literary point of view and the notes and introductions especially in the "uncut" edition are extremely helpful.

The New American Bible (NAB), also under Catholic auspices, appeared in 1970 after a long history. An outstanding achievement of American biblical scholars, it stands somewhere between the literal quality of the RSV and the freer, literary style of the JBE.

Different from any of the above is *The Living Bible*. This is a paraphrase rather than a translation. Its author, Kenneth Taylor, is a minister who worked for years to produce an easy reading Bible. He defines his purpose as "to say as exactly as possible what the authors of the Scriptures meant, and to say it simply, expanding where necessary for a clear understanding by the modern reader." This work has been published under Catholic sponsorship with the title, *The Way: Catholic Edition.* Some scholars have expressed serious reservations about the fact that the words of Scripture are pressed into the author's own theological mold, sometimes resulting in misleading and inaccurate readings.

Catholics who hear the reading of the Scriptures at the celebration of the Eucharist are generally listening to either the Revised Standard Version, or the Jerusalem Bible, or the New American Bible. Most American liturgical books use one of these three translations.

A WORD TO THE OLD TIMERS

Why the flurry of new translations, at least by Catholic scholars?

For almost two hundred years, Catholics had gotten used to hearing the same Gospels in the same words Sunday after Sunday. The language and style had become familiar, fitting like an old shoe.

The translation that formed the biblical knowledge of the English-speaking Catholic world from the middle of the 18th to the middle of the 20th century was a revision made by Bishop Challoner of an earlier Catholic translation known as the Douay-Rheims from the two cities where the translation was made from 1582 to 1609.

These translations were actually translations of translations. At the end of the fourth and beginning of the fifth centuries, St. Jerome put large portions of the Old Testament into Latin, which was then the spoken language. A Latin translation of the New Testament was added. This Bible of Jerome's eventually designated the "Vulgate" or "common version," served as the Bible of the western World until the Protestant Reformation.

But Latin passed from the scene as a living, spoken language as modern languages developed. When Catholics did the natural thing of translating the Bible into the new languages, they went to Jerome's Latin version rather than to the original languages of the Bible, the Hebrew, Aramaic and Greek of the Old Testament and the Greek of the New.

Protestant translators early returned to the original languages. However, not until the 20th century did papal directives give the impetus and approval to Catholic scholars to make their translations from the original texts rather than from the Vulgate.

The reason for this emphasis on the Vulgate, especially as it was manifested by the Council of Trent (1546) was the confusing situation that faced the teacher and preacher.

Many different versions of the Bible were being used by Catholics. These versions were not different because anyone intended them to be so but simply because mistakes, variations, interpretations creeping into the text made them so. Things had gotten so bad some centuries earlier that a center of learning, the University of Paris, had to pick out one version of the translation and decree that it and only it could be used. Each student came to the University from his particular corner of Europe with his own Bible under his arm. Each of these Bibles was supposedly the same – Jerome's translation. Yet changes in the course of copying his translation had so snow-balled that getting a common starting point in theology from the Scriptures was all but impossible.

The Council of Trent faced this same situation. The only text of the Bible generally available was Jerome's translation, even with the variety in different versions of it. The Council decreed that this translation should be put in the best order possible, that scholars should decide which was the correct reading of all passages where there was variety, that a standardized Vulgate should be published.

The Council never intended to define that the Vulgate had more authority than the original texts. It was trying to get control of a chaotic situation in preaching and teaching arising from the lack of a Bible on whose text and readings all could agree.

For many reasons, this situation lasted through 1943 when Pope Pius XII encouraged the making of translations from the original languages. This stance was echoed by Vatican II.

Hence, the multiplication of translations into English in recent years, all from the original languages of the Bible instead of from the Latin translation of St. Jerome.

SUGGESTIONS FOR REFLECTION

1. Have you ever copied something incorrectly?
Have you ever heard wrongly something that was said to you?
Have you ever made a mistake because of fatigue or illness?
What were the consequences to yourself or others because
of any of these errors?

2. Do the errors that occurred in the copying of the Scriptures reflect on God and his ability to give us the truth?
The mistakes happened through human error.
How are they corrected? How sure are we that the Bible as we have it now is the Bible as it was written?

3. Have you ever tried to translate a statement or question from one language to another (e. g. Latin to English, or English to Latin, etc.)?
Was it easy to make the meaning exactly clear in the second language? Can you understand how two people might translate the same passage differently?

4. In the Church, we have had many translations of the Bible into English.
What are the major differences between the King James version, the Douay version, and the new readings used at Mass? Have you met persons who wonder why a new translation was needed? How would you explain the history of Bible translations to help such persons be more at home with the new translations? Have you found the new translations more helpful in your understanding of the message?

CHAPTER VI

ALL OR NOTHING AT ALL

These final remarks are addressed to extremists at opposite
ends of a line. The extremists will constitute a small part
of those who might read the Bible. But by dealing with
them, something might become clearer to the average person
who started reading this book to get ready to study the Bible,
and is still waiting to begin.

THE BIBLE SAYS EVERYTHING

"This is what the words of the Bible say; therefore this is
what the words of the Bible mean. Everything the Bible
says is to be taken at face value with no meddling or 'interpreting' by men. And furthermore, the Bible is all that any
man needs to face and answer the issues of life."

This approach refuses to take either God or the Bible
seriously.

God has indeed worked through men living and dying in
the course of human history. This action of God reached
its unique high point in the life and teaching, death and
resurrection of Jesus.

This action of God was experienced, witnessed and interpreted by communities and individuals in the communities
who formed, collected, preserved, wrote and edited the
material in the Scriptures. They were men of their time.
They shared the thought patterns of their time. They
reflected the education they had received. They spoke to

the problems and issues that confronted them.

To expect to be able to pick up the Bible and read and understand it perfectly without further study is like visiting a foreign land and expecting to understand everything simply because one has bought a phrase-book of foreign words. How much is missed because the traveller is not familiar with the customs, the language, the way of life in that land!

Visitors to the Near East often find it difficult to adjust to the haggling over prices that still goes on in some areas. The prospective buyer notes a trinket that he would be willing to pay $5.00 for. No price can be found on the article. When asked, the shop-keeper indicates that the article sells for $50.00.

In shock, the shopper staggers to the door, only to have the proprietor call after him, "Never mind! "

My own first reaction in such a situation was, "What do you mean 'Never mind? ' It's my money! " I took "Never mind" in its common English equivalent of "That's none of your business," or "Don't pay any attention." My $50.00 was certainly my business and I certainly would pay attention. Only by experience did I learn that "Never mind! " in this context really should be translated as, "Okay! Ignore that price. Let's get down to some real bargaining."

Without the knowledge of culture, of background, of methods of buying and selling, I was a stranger misunderstanding even those who spoke the same language as I.

Expecting the words of the Bible to be completely clear and meaningful without taking into account the times they came from, the men responsible for them, the forms of literature represented, demands that God work a miracle of understanding for every man who in the course of centuries will open its covers. This sells short the truth in

John's profession that the "Word became flesh." God's
Word, both when lived and spoken in history and in its
fullest expression in Jesus, assumed full human characteristics.

To understand God's word, we must be able to use all the
disciplines that are the key to unlocking the treasures of the
Bible; language study, archeology, history, etc.

Perhaps this seems to raise an impossible problem for the
believer. No one person can be archeologist, language
scholar, historian, preacher, teacher, all at the same time.
The job is too big!

This is precisely why we belong to and trust in a community of faith. In our community of faith, the Church, all
kinds of people ranging from the scholar to the teacher
to the believer facing the questions of life offer their
contributions to the common task of understanding God
through the Bible.

To ignore the reality that Paul teaches when he refers to
the community as the "Body of Christ," as the living
presence of the Word of God today, is to refuse to accept
the way God has chosen to act among us.

THE BIBLE SAYS NOTHING

"The Bible is dead. Its language, its style, its form, its
examples, its history, its science, are long out of style. It
is not relevant. It says nothing to modern man. Why waste
time on the ideas of the past, as significant as they may
have been for their own time? "

People who think this way are like the person who claims
that the Bible says everything, except that they have gone
to the other extreme. They are not willing or able to take
the effort, in union with the living community, to examine
the Scriptures, to reflect on them. They have gotten lost
in the quest for instant relevance. The danger is that this

relevant system becomes staler than last month's cake as soon as the circumstances of life change.

Whatever the relevant language or system, if its language and questions speak only to the problems of the moment, it soon passes out of style.

No matter how much he develops, how much life whizzes by filled with new gadgets, new scientific instruments, new powers rising and falling on the political scene, man is still thrown back into facing certain key issues that never go out of style.

What does my life mean?   What is its purpose?   Where am I going?   Is there anything beyond man and what he can see?   If so, is this "beyond," this future open to man?

These questions were being asked in the earliest literatures that men have recorded.   They are being asked today. There is no indication that they will ever cease being of vital concern because they get to the heart of the matter.

With these issues the Bible deals. It tells of God's involvement in human affairs to reveal himself as the goal and purpose of life. It tells that this goal is something man can work for in hope and look forward to with joy. It tells that man desperately needs God, that God is a loving Father eager to respond to that need. It teaches that life makes sense, even through moments of nonsense; that life has purpose, even through moments of wandering; that life leads to good, even through moments of evil.

SUGGESTIONS FOR REFLECTION

1. This book has attempted to introduce the reader to the development and history of the Bible.
Do you think it could help Catholics to become more interested in and less fearful of reading the Bible?   Do we, as a community of faith, have a responsibility to help

people face the questions of life with better understanding of God through the Bible? What specifically could you do to bring this about with the people with whom you live and work?

2. How does God use us to act and speak as members of the "Body of Christ," as the "living presence of the Word of God today," in our world of the twentieth century?

3. Some fundamentalists quote and interpret *literally* all of the Bible. For example, they claim to know the exact date of the end of the world, and they believe the Bible forbids anyone but God to be called "Father."

After reading this book, how could you explain the way Catholics believe in the meaning of Scripture?

4. There are persons today in business, science, technology, and social work who think of the Bible as ancient history, without meaning for our times. They do not reflect on the "why" of human life, but throw themselves into the "how," getting the most out of day-to-day life. Why is it as important to reflect on the "why" of life as it is to reflect on the "how"?

5. Have you found answers for the meaning of you life in reflecting on Scripture? Do you consider the Bible to be timeless?

SUGGESTIONS FOR FURTHER READING

J. Becker, *The Formation of the Old Testament.* Chicago:
Franciscan Herald Press (Herald Biblical Booklets), 1972
(paperback).

R. Brown *et al., The Jerome Biblical Commentary.* Englewood
Cliffs, N.J.: Prentice-Hall, 1968. Articles on "Inspiration and
Inerrancy," "Canonicity," "Texts and Versions," "Hermeneu-
tics."

W. Harrington, *Record of Revelation: The Bible.* Chicago:
Priory Press, 1965.

J. McKenzie, *Dictionary of the Bible.* Milwaukee: Bruce, 1965
(paperback). Articles on "Canon," "History, Historical Writing,"
"Inspiration," "Interpretation," "Text," "English Versions of
the Bible," "Vulgate."

Vatican II, *Dogmatic Constitution on Divine Revelation (Dei Ver-
bum).*

Understanding the New Testament

Howard Mark Kee